THE ULTIMATE GUIDE TO COOKING VEGETABLES

THE INDIAN WAY

Prasenjeet Kumar and Sonali Kumar

Disclaimers

Although the Authors have made every effort to ensure that the information in this book was correct at the time of publication, the Authors do not assume and hereby disclaim any liability to any party for any loss, damage, or disruption caused by errors or omissions, whether such errors or omissions result from negligence, accident, or any other cause.

This book is not intended as a substitute for the medical advice of physicians. The reader should regularly consult a physician in matters relating to his/her health and particularly with respect to any symptoms that may require diagnosis or medical attention.

This book also assumes that the reader does not suffer from any food allergies or related medical conditions. Readers suffering from food allergies are requested to skip the recipes that contains ingredients which trigger adverse reactions in that reader or in his/her family and friends.

The spellings used in this book are British, which may look strange to our American friends, but NOT to those living in Australia, Canada, India, Ireland and, of course, the United Kingdom. This means that color is written as colour and so on. We hope that is NOT too confusing!

Table of Contents

Let my words, like vegetables, be tender and sweet, for tomorrow I may have to eat them.

—Unknown

Why Veggies

 don't want any vegetables, thank you. I paid for the cow to eat them for me."

—Douglas Coupland

"Vegetarians, and their Hezbollah-like splinter faction, the vegans ... are the enemy of everything good and decent in the human spirit."

—Anthony Bourdain

Ah! If you agreed, even remotely, with these somewhat conceited observations, it's time you opened your eyes to another, startling and fascinating, side of vegetables.

Veggies fight diseases

There is no question that people who eat fruit and vegetables regularly have a drastically reduced risk of contracting many chronic diseases. U.S. Department of Agriculture (on its ChooseMyPlate.gov website) lists a number of reasons as to why you should make at least half your plate full of fruits and vegetables:

* Vegetables are low in calories and fats but are high in vitamins and minerals like calcium, magnesium, potassium, iron, beta-carotene, vitamin B-complex, vitamin-C, vitamin-A, and vitamin K.

* Unlike meats or eggs, vegetables contain NIL cholesterol. According to EarthSave, the average vegetarian has about ¼, and pure vegans have less than 1/10, the chance of having a heart attack as the average non vegetarian.

* Vegetables don't expose you to so many preservatives, antibiotics and hormones, which are common in meat and are linked to cancer.

* Vegetables abound in antioxidants. These phyto-chemicals help, first, to protect you from oxidant stress, diseases, and cancers. Second, to boost your immunity to fight these if you unfortunately do get affected. And third to improve blood sugar levels in people at risk for diabetes.

* Believe it or not, vegetables also promote hair growth. In fact they can give your hair a greater health boost than the most expensive shampoos you can afford. This is because vegetables are packed with the vitamins and minerals that your hair needs the most.

* Additionally, vegetables are packed with dietary fibre such as cellulose, mucilage, hemi-cellulose,

gums, and pectin that are known as non-starch polysaccharides (NSP). These substances reduce blood cholesterol levels, absorb excess water in the colon, and aid the waste matter's smooth passage out of the body. Thus, dietary fibre protects you from conditions like chronic constipation, diverticulosis, haemorrhoids, colon cancer, irritable bowel syndrome, and rectal fissures.

N.B. Do consult your doctor, however, if you have a damaged intestinal lining, because a high-fibre diet in that case can cause bloating and other complications.

Veggies make you fitter

Recently, vegetables have caught the attention of the fitness conscious because they are so very low in calories. For example, Celery per 100 gram has just 16 calories. Vegetables like bottle gourd, cabbage, bok-choy, eggplant, spinach, etc have all less than 20 calories per 100 gram.

There is another great benefit which food scientists vouch for. Veggies increase our BMR or Basal Metabolism Rate because they make us spend more energy to digest them than what we get out of them.

So when you eat vegetables, you may lose more weight than you would gain! That puts veggies on the top of the list for "negative calorie foods" that many nutritionists are going gaga about.

Finally, vegetables contain high levels of water naturally. The more you consume vegetables, therefore, the more would be your water intake. This would not only help you hydrate better but also help flush out waste products and toxins from your body.

Now that we have agreed that veggies are good for us, the next question is how much should they be in our daily diet.

Let's once again go to the US Federal dietary guidelines. These now recommend at least nine servings of vegetables and fruits per day. Seasonal vegetables are encouraged. If they are local and organic, all the better.

How should you buy vegetables?

Savvy vegetable lovers recommend that:

* While shopping for veggies, buy small quantities so that they can be used up within a day or two.

* Always buy fresh veggies that are bright in colour and flavour and feel heavy in your hands.

* Try to avoid veggies that are crushed, spoilt or have spots or moulds.

* To the extent possible, buy whole vegetables instead of cut-and-cleaned versions. The latter although more convenient would have considerably less nutrition than whole veggies.

* If you cut and leave vegetables, oxidation will occur and they will be somewhat discoloured. You can stop this oxidation by adding ascorbic acid or by refrigerating the vegetables. In general, cut veggies should be put inside zip pouches and stored in the main compartment (and NOT the freezer) of your fridge and used up as quickly as possible.

* Do wash your veggies thoroughly. You could rinse them in salt water, and gently swish in cool water till you are satisfied that they are free from dirt, sand and pesticides.

* If you need to store whole veggies, place them inside the vegetable compartment of your fridge. Do try to store vegetables separate from raw meats like poultry, meat, fish, or seafood. You can wrap vegetables in perforated plastic or porous paper such as newspaper and then refrigerate them, which increases their shelf life. But if you use newspaper, see that the vegetables are not wet, because the ink from the newspaper then could stick to the vegetables!

Do try to eat a rainbow every day

Ah, you can't do this with meats, can you? Even if you made a distinction between red and white meats?

Yes, because face it, every meat would more or less be a shade of pink!

Experts advise that you should try to eat 4-5 different types of vegetables every day. The more varied and colourful your plate be, the more extensive would be the benefits to your health. The rich colour of veggies not just soothe your eyes but contribute some unique and important micronutrients.

So to have on your plate:

* RED: You could consider tomato, red pepper, beets, and red onions. The shiny outer skins of red pepper have a high percentage of silica that helps maintain your hair's thickness. Tomatoes contain lycopene, which protects you from vision problems and shields your skin from the harmful rays of the sun. Interestingly, cooked tomatoes offer you more lycopene than raw ones, meaning you get more benefits from having tomato sauce than raw tomatoes!

* ORANGE/YELLOW: You could introduce carrots, orange peppers, sweet potato, and yellow pumpkin. These have lots of vitamin C, which protects collagen. Collagen retains the elasticity of your skin, thus delaying the appearance of wrinkles. Vitamin C, considered as the "anti-aging vitamin", also aids in iron absorption, helps heal cuts and wounds and keeps teeth and gums healthy. Sweet potatoes have potassium which helps to maintain healthy blood pressure.

* GREEN: There is plenty of choice here. You could include leafy veggies like spinach, kale, mustard leaves, okra, avocado, asparagus, artichoke, bok choy, green cabbage, Chinese cabbage, broccoli,

green pepper, coriander or cilantro leaves, basil, parsley, mint etc. Dark green vegetables have a bioflavonoid known as "Quercetin" which has anti-cancer and anti-allergen properties. Leafy veggies like spinach are also full of Vitamin A that keeps eyes and skin healthy. Cabbage, Brussels sprouts, and broccoli contain indoles and isothiocyanates which protect against all kinds of cancers like colon cancer, breast cancer, skin cancer, etc. Most greens are high in magnesium and have a low glycaemic index, which helps people with type 2 diabetes.

It is in fact recommended that if you eat at least 1 serving of green leafy vegetables each day, it will considerably lower the risks of diabetes. The high level of vitamin K helps in the production of osteocalcin, a protein mandatory for proper bone health that helps decrease the chances of hip fractures in middle-aged women. Avocados are full of potassium, glutathione, healthy fats, and more Folate (folic acid) than any other fruit. Folate is extremely important for babies, when they are in their mothers' wombs, as this reduces the risk of neural tube defects, spina bifida, and anencephaly during foetal development. Asparagus is also rich in folate.

* BLUE/PURPLE: Here you could consider including eggplant, and purple cabbage. Eggplants are rich in antioxidants like nasunin that protects your brain cells from damage. Purple veggies are also loaded with fibre and potassium which reduce the risk of stroke and dementia.

* WHITE: You could include garlic, cauliflower, onions, ginger, radishes, mushrooms, etc. The allyl sulphides found in garlic, onions, and shallots help in lowering high blood pressure and protecting the stomach and digestive tract from cancer. Onions are also loaded with a peptide called GPCS which slows your body's loss of calcium.

How to match the benefits of a non-vegetarian diet

According to veganoutreach.org, Americans consume 2,714 land animals in their lifetime. The typical American plate is supposed to be 50% animal protein, 25% overcooked vegetables and 25% starch like white potatoes. Experts advise that you recreate your plate by shifting to 50% plant foods like vegetables (or some fruit), 25% lean protein (like fish) and 25% whole grain.

Nutritionally, if you have decided to eat less animal products, you should ensure that your diet is high in protein-rich vegetables to compensate for the proteins and amino acids that meats have. So you would need to eat plenty of beans and spinach, along with whole grain wheat and rice for a balanced meal. You would also need to add some soy protein, which is the only protein of vegetarian origin that can match the benefits that you get from animal proteins.

Scientifically, it is established that apart from "first-class" proteins, non-vegetarian diets also contain more iron, zinc, calcium, and vitamin B-12 than vegetarian dishes. Plant sources like spinach do contain plenty of iron, but in a non-heme form. This is more sensitive to inhibitors than the iron that you get from meats. So if you wish to increase your blood-iron levels, you should not only consume more plant iron, but also avoid absorption inhibitors, like tea or coffee.

Similarly, for Zinc, you should consume more of soybeans, cashews, and sunflower seeds, and reduce your intake of inhibitors.

For getting more calcium from vegetarian meals, the strategy would be to avoid veggies that are high in oxalates as they will inhibit calcium absorption. That's why dietitians suggest that vegetarians do not consume too much of spinach, beet greens, or Swiss chard, as the calcium component of a meal plan, because while they are rich in calcium, they also contain high amounts of oxalates. Instead vegetarians should consider other options, such as soy yogurt, tofu, beans, almonds, and calcium-fortified foods.

The biggest challenge, however, is about getting Vitamin B-12, because it does not exist naturally in any non-animal form. In that case, it would be prudent to take suitable supplements or vitamin B-12 fortified foods, such as certain soy milks and cereals.

The idea of discussing the above "shortcomings" is simply that when planned well, a vegetarian diet cannot only make up for what it lacks (when compared to a non-vegetarian diet), but it can also far exceed the health quotient of most non-vegetarian diets.

Phew! There is a lot that can be said about vegetables. The short point is that if you succeed in including them in your daily diet, despite the cultural baggage you may have, your body will thank you for that.

As to how you can do that in the tastiest manner possible, may we look at how the Indians do that?

You need to go then to the next chapter.

A Thought for the Day

"Better to eat vegetables and fear no creditors, than eat duck and hide from them."

–The Talmud

Cooking Veggies the Indian way

*"**T**omatoes and oregano make it Italian; wine and tarragon make it French. Sour cream makes it Russian; lemon and cinnamon make it Greek. Soy sauce makes it Chinese; garlic makes it good."*

–Alice May Brock

Ah, as usual, the lady forgot about the Indians!

But probably she was not referring to veggies at all. Because if she did, she would have to acknowledge that no one cooks vegetables as well and in as many ways as the Indians do.

For pure vegetarians India is just heaven. Vegetables are an integral part of Indian cuisine and Indians consume them in several ways. Displaying an amazing mix of tastes and aromas, Indian cuisine is perhaps the most wonderful, varied, robust, and sensual of all the cuisines in the world when it comes to vegetarianism. No wonder, the Indian prowess in whipping up an amazing vegetarian meal, even from the most bitter of vegetables (like *karela* or the bitter gourd), is now appreciated around the globe.

The traditional Indian cuisine is based on matching and mixing unusual and unique flavours. This technique of incorporating more than 10 ingredients jointly is what makes Indian food stand out from the other cuisines.

Indian restaurants, within and outside India, are doing a wonderful job of popularising traditional Indian cooking but with a contemporary touch, especially in their methods of presentation. For example, many Indian restaurants now serve their cuisines in well engraved "*kadhais*" or in the "*Thali*" or Indian meal platter format. The cultural surroundings too of these restaurants introduce diners to Indian architecture, heritage and traditions. This lends a touch of authenticity to the cuisine that is served within the four walls of such restaurants.

Traditional Indian food still maintains its uniqueness regardless of the cultural shifts or the use of modern equipment. Many celebrity chefs have succeeded in redefining Indian cuisine but without sacrificing its ethnicity. This has no doubt added to the novelty and charm of Indian cuisine.

Unlike other countries, which have probably 3-4 cuisines at the max, India is a subcontinent which is a mixture of many culinary traditions. Hence it would be difficult for anyone to classify any one regional food of India as representative of the entire Indian cuisine. Indian culture symbolizes diversity, and this feature is well depicted in the food preparation of each state.

Broadly, in India, there appear to be three distinct ways of cooking veggies. First, the North Indian way that uses *garam masala*, or a medley of aromatic spices like cardamom, cinnamon, cloves, etc. Second, the East Indian way that uses *pachphoran*, or a mixture of five other spices that don't make up *garam masala*. And then, there is the South Indian version that neither uses *garam masala* nor *pachforan* but displays a totally different way of making veggies by using black mustard seeds, curry leaves, and coconut.

In between we have the Western India cuisine which sometimes borrows elements from South India but adds its own unique ingredients, like *Kokum* in the Konkan region, which are not used by any other cuisine in India.

All four versions are absolutely mouth-watering. I am sure you can't say the same about most of the Western or even Oriental vegetable dishes, which to the Indian palate tastes like "salad". Unless you use chicken stock or fish sauce to impart some taste or flavour. But then, that won't make them "pure vegetarian", would they?

Indians are also unique in using pressure cookers for cooking their veggies and lentils. This no doubt economises on the use of fuel or electricity. But it also, because of the high temperatures it generates, destroys bugs that may lurk unseen in the folds of your vegetables. This book, therefore, unabashedly gives the recipes for cooking with pressure cookers.

However, please don't despair if you, for whatever reason, have NOT yet invested in a pressure cooker. Instead, if you are comfortable with the use of woks/deep sauce pans, we have provided the option for cooking with the latter too, with the adjusted cooking time.

Kitchen equipment is constantly evolving, and it is difficult to adapt such an ancient cuisine as Indian to all such fancy devices. Still wherever possible, we have tried to use rice cookers or air fryers in the interest of faster, easier or lower calorie cooking.

With this brief introduction, I now present 101 mouth-watering 100% vegetarian recipes. There are 26 curries, 24 dry recipes, 10 recipes for cooking veggies with rice or breads, and 19 kinds of snacks and accompaniments.

For the spice-challenged or nostalgia ridden folks, there are 14 dishes from the days of the British Raj that do use cheese and involve baking, if you were missing that!

And finally there are 8 desserts you can make from veggies. I'm sure you didn't think of that, did you?

So forget your boring boiled and broiled and baked ways to make veggie dishes and let this new book open your eyes to the wonderful possibilities of cooking vegetables the way northern, southern, eastern and western Indians do.

And the bottom line is that you master these and you can handle any Indian vegetable dish from any part of India, I promise.

N.B. Please remember that the "Home Style" recipes I have catalogued here are made regularly in my home. You are strongly encouraged to experiment, adapt and add your own variation so that the food tastes like your "Home food".

Chapter 1: Snacks & Accompaniments

"At lunch you order steamed vegetables because you're remembering that you have a heart too. You feel humbled by your heart, it works so hard. You want to thank it. You give your heart a little pat."

–Aimee Bender, The Girl in the Flammable Skirt

Starters or side dishes in India don't mean rice or boiled corn, because rice or *rotis* occupy quite a pride of place on the main platter.

Instead they would include *Pakoras* (vegetable fritters) or *Chiura/Poha* (savoury rice flakes) that you get served when you visit someone's home in North India. In wayside eateries, you may also see some *Aloo* (potato) or *Paneer* (cottage cheese) *Tikkis* (cutlets) being sizzled on huge pans.

On the other hand, Indian accompaniments are those chutneys (sauces), *raitas* (yoghurt based dish), *papadams*, and pickles without which an Indian *thali* (platter) would be considered incomplete. You basically take a bite of these in between your main meal to wake up your taste buds and to cleanse your palate, so to say.

If you crave for any of these sinful snacks, sauces and accompaniments, then do read on for some really idiot proof recipes.

We present 19 gems: 6 types of *Pakoras*, 2 *Tikkis*, 2 grilled snacks, 3 veggie kebabs, 3 chutneys and 3 *raitas*.

Pakoras (Vegetable Fritters

Please note that most *pakoras* would look similar (i.e. like fried dumplings) whether you make it of onions, spinach, cauliflower, potato, or bottle gourd.

Vegetable Fritters are a very popular snack to be eaten along with a nice hot cup of tea especially on a cool rainy day. All kinds of vegetables can be used for this tasty snack. We present some six of the most popular ones.

Onion *Pakoras*

Ingredients

Chick pea flour-1 cup

Rice flour-1/2 cup

Baking powder-1/2 teaspoon

Asafoetida (*Hing*)-1/2 teaspoon

Coriander (*Dhania*) powder-1 teaspoon

Cumin seeds (*Jeera*)-1/2 teaspoon

Turmeric (*Haldi*)-1/2 teaspoon

Kashmiri Red Chilli powder–1/2 tea spoon (Recommended for colour, but if you like your dish to be really spicy, use some other hotter red chilli powder)

Salt-1/2 teaspoon or to taste

Water-1 cup (approximately)

Sliced (and peeled) Onions-4

Oil for deep frying (quantity would depend on the size of your wok)

Method

Leaving out the onions and the oil, mix all the other ingredients well.

Add the water and beat until smooth and light. The batter should be of a thin coating consistency.

Set it aside for at least 15 minutes. This helps the flour to absorb the water well and attain a thicker consistency.

If it becomes too thick, you may add a little more water and beat well.

Now add the onions to this batter.

Heat oil in a frying pan or wok.

When the oil starts smoking, take the mixture with the onion slices, a tablespoonful at a time, and drop into the hot oil.

Be careful of the splatter that follows.

You will find that the fritters swell up.

Gently turn them around and take out from the oil when they are nice and golden brown. Remove to a dish which is covered with a paper napkin to help absorb all the excess oil.

Repeat till all the fritters/*pakoras* are fried.

Enjoy with any of the chutneys, especially the mint chutney.

Prep time: 20 minutes

Cooking time: 3 minutes @ each batch

Total time: Approximately 30 minutes

Paneer Pakoras (Cottage Cheese fritters)

Ingredients

Chick pea flour-1 cup

Rice flour-1/2 cup

Baking powder-1/2 teaspoon

Asafoetida (*Hing*)-1/2 teaspoon

Coriander (*Dhania*) powder-1 teaspoon

Cumin seeds (*Jeera*)-1/2 teaspoon

Turmeric (*Haldi*) powder-1/2 teaspoon

Kashmiri Red Chilli powder–1/2 tea spoon (Recommended for colour, but if you like your dish to be really spicy, use some other hotter red chilli powder)

Salt-1/2 teaspoon or to taste

Water-1 cup (approximately)

Paneer (Cottage Cheese)-300 grams (10oz) (1 cup) cut into bite size pieces

Oil for deep frying (quantity would depend on the size of your wok)

Method

Leaving out the *paneer* and the oil, mix all the other ingredients well.

Add the water and beat until smooth and light. The batter should be of a thin coating consistency.

Set it aside for at least 15 minutes. This helps the flour to absorb the water well and attain a thicker consistency.

If it becomes too thick, you may add a little more water and beat well.

Now add the *paneer* pieces to this batter.

Heat oil in a frying pan or wok.

When the oil starts smoking, take the mixture with the *paneer* pieces, a tablespoonful at a time, and drop into the hot oil.

Be careful of the splatter that follows.

You will find that the fritters swell up.

Gently turn them around and take out from the oil when they are nice and golden brown.

Remove to a dish which is covered with a paper napkin to help absorb all the excess oil.

Repeat till all the fritters/*pakoras* are fried.

Enjoy with any of the chutneys, especially the mint chutney.

Prep time: 20 minutes

Cooking time: 3 minutes @ each batch

Total time: Approximately 30 minutes

Palak Pakoras (Spinach fritters)

Ingredients

Chick pea flour-1 cup

Rice flour-1/2 cup

Baking powder-1/2 teaspoon

Asafoetida (*Hing*)-1/2 teaspoon

Coriander (*Dhania*) powder-1 teaspoon

Cumin seeds (*Jeera*)-1/2 teaspoon

Turmeric (*Haldi*) powder-1/2 teaspoon

Kashmiri Red Chilli powder–1/2 tea spoon (Recommended for colour, but if you like your dish to be really spicy, use some other hotter red chilli powder)

Salt-1/2 teaspoon or to taste

Water-1 cup (approximately)

Spinach (only leaves)-300 grams (10oz) (1 cup)

Oil for deep frying (quantity would depend on the size of your wok)

Method

Leaving out the spinach and the oil, mix all the other ingredients well.

Add the water and beat until smooth and light. The batter should be of a thin coating consistency.

Set it aside for at least 15 minutes. This helps the flour to absorb the water well and attain a thicker consistency.

If it becomes too thick, you may add a little more water and beat well.

Now add the spinach to this batter.

Heat oil in a frying pan or wok.

When the oil starts smoking, take the mixture with the spinach, one leaf at a time, and drop into the hot oil.

Be careful of the splatter that follows.

You will find that the fritters swell up.

Gently turn them around and take out from the oil when they are nice and golden brown.

Remove to a dish which is covered with a paper napkin to help absorb all the excess oil.

Repeat till all the fritters/*pakoras* are fried.

Enjoy with any of the chutneys, especially the mint chutney.

Prep time: 20 minutes

Cooking time: 3 minutes @ each batch

Total time: Approximately 30 minutes

Gobi Pakoras (Cauliflower Fritters)

Ingredients

Chick pea flour-1 cup

Rice flour-1/2 cup

Baking powder-1/2 teaspoon

Asafoetida (*Hing*)-1/2 teaspoon

Coriander (*Dhania*) powder-1 teaspoon

Cumin seeds (*Jeera*)-1/2 teaspoon

Turmeric (*Haldi*) powder-1/2 teaspoon

Kashmiri Red Chilli powder–1/2 tea spoon (Recommended for colour, but if you like your dish to be really spicy, use some other hotter red chilli powder)

Salt-1/2 teaspoon or to taste

Water-1 cup (approximately)

Cauliflower-1 (with florets separated into bite size pieces)

Oil for deep frying (quantity would depend on the size of your wok)

Method

Leaving out the cauliflower and the oil, mix all the other ingredients well.

Add the water and beat until smooth and light. The batter should be of a thin coating consistency.

Set it aside for at least 15 minutes. This helps the flour to absorb the water well and attain a thicker consistency.

If it becomes too thick, you may add a little more water and beat well.

Now add the cauliflower pieces to this batter.

Heat oil in a frying pan or wok.

When the oil starts smoking, take the mixture with the cauliflower pieces, a tablespoonful at a time, and drop into the hot oil.

Be careful of the splatter that follows.

You will find that the fritters swell up.

Gently turn them around and take out from the oil when they are nice and golden brown.

Remove to a dish which is covered with a paper napkin to help absorb all the excess oil.

Repeat till all the fritters/*pakoras* are fried.

Enjoy with any of the chutneys, especially the mint chutney.

Prep time: 20 minutes

Cooking time: 3 minutes @ each batch

Total time: Approximately 30 minutes

***Baingan Pakoras* (Aubergine Fritters)**

Ingredients

Chick pea flour-1 cup

Rice flour-1/2 cup

Baking powder-1/2 teaspoon

Asafoetida (*Hing*)-1/2 teaspoon

Coriander (*Dhania*) powder-1 teaspoon

Cumin seeds (*Jeera*)-1/2 teaspoon

Turmeric (*Haldi*) powder-1/2 teaspoon

Kashmiri Red Chilli powder–1/2 tea spoon (Recommended for colour, but if you like your dish to be really spicy, use some other hotter red chilli powder)

Salt-1/2 teaspoon or to taste

Water-1 cup (approximately)

Round big Aubergines-2 (thinly sliced)

Oil for deep frying (quantity would depend on the size of your wok)

Method

Leaving out the aubergines and the oil, mix all the other ingredients well.

Add the water and beat until smooth and light. The batter should be of a thin coating consistency.

Set it aside for at least 15 minutes. This helps the flour to absorb the water well and attain a thicker consistency.

If it becomes too thick, you may add a little more water and beat well.

Now add the aubergine slices to this batter.

Heat oil in a frying pan or wok.

When the oil starts smoking, take the mixture with the aubergine slices, a slice at a time, and drop into the hot oil.

Be careful of the splatter that follows.

You will find that the fritters swell up.

Gently turn them around and take out from the oil when they are nice and golden brown.

Remove to a dish which is covered with a paper napkin to help absorb all the excess oil.

Repeat till all the fritters/*pakoras* are fried.

Enjoy with any of the chutneys, especially the mint chutney.

Prep time: 20 minutes

Cooking time: 3 minutes @ each batch

Total time: Approximately 30 minutes

Aloo Pakoras (Potato Fritters)

Ingredients

Chick pea flour-1 cup

Rice flour-1/2 cup

Baking powder-1/2 teaspoon

Asafoetida (*Hing*)-1/2 teaspoon

Coriander (*Dhania)* powder-1 teaspoon

Cumin seeds (*Jeera*)-1/2 teaspoon

Turmeric (*Haldi*) powder-1/2 teaspoon

Kashmiri Red Chilli powder–1/2 tea spoon (Recommended for colour, but if you like your dish to be really spicy, use some other hotter red chilli powder)

Salt-1/2 teaspoon or to taste

Water-1 cup (approximately)

Potatoes-4 (thinly sliced)

Oil for deep frying (quantity would depend on the size of your wok)

Method

Leaving out the potato and the oil, mix all the other ingredients well.

Add the water and beat until smooth and light. The batter should be of a thin coating consistency.

Set it aside for at least 15 minutes. This helps the flour to absorb the water well and attain a thicker consistency.

If it becomes too thick, you may add a little more water and beat well.

Now add the potato slices to this batter.

Heat oil in a frying pan or wok.

When the oil starts smoking, take the mixture with the potato slices, a slice at a time, and drop into the hot oil.

Be careful of the splatter that follows.

You will find that the fritters swell up.

Gently turn them around and take out from the oil when they are nice and golden brown.

Remove to a dish which is covered with a paper napkin to help absorb all the excess oil.

Repeat till all the fritters/*pakoras* are fried.

Enjoy with any of the chutneys, especially the mint chutney.

Prep time: 20 minutes

Cooking time: 3 minutes @ each batch

Total time: Approximately 30 minutes

Aloo Tikki (Potato Cutlets Indian style)

Ingredients

Boiled potatoes-500 grams (18oz) (2 cups)

Bread pieces-2

Chopped Onion-1

Green chillies (chopped and de-seeded)-2

Cumin seeds (*Jeera*)-1/2 teaspoon

Chopped Fresh Coriander (*Dhania*) Leaves-A small bunch

Lemon juice-1 tablespoon

Salt- ½ teaspoon or to taste

Cooking Oil-2 tablespoon

Method

Mash the boiled potatoes well.

Soak the bread pieces in water. Squeeze the water from the bread with both hands and then add to the boiled potatoes.

Add all the other ingredients and mix well.

Shape the mashed potato mixture into small flat patties.

In a shallow non-stick pan, heat the cooking oil and place the patties.

Brown the patties evenly on both sides and remove to a dish covered with an absorbent paper napkin.

Repeat till all the patties are cooked.

Serve hot with chutneys.

Prep time: 5 minutes

Cooking time: 3 minutes (Even if you are roasting more patties, each will still take 3 minutes to brown).

Total time: 8 minutes

Paneer Tikki (Cottage Cheese Patties)

Ingredients

Paneer (Cottage Cheese)-500 grams (18oz) (2 cups)

Bread pieces-2

Chopped Onion-1

Green chillies (chopped and de-seeded)-2

Cumin seeds (*Jeera*)-1/2 teaspoon

Chopped Fresh Coriander (*Dhania*) Leaves-A small bunch

Sugar-1/2 teaspoon

Garam Masala (mixture of common Indian spices) crushed- 1/2 tea spoon

Tip: If you can't get ready-made *garam masala* mixture from a nearby Indian store, you can make yours by using 1 black cardamom, 3 green cardamoms, 4 cloves, and 1 inch cinnamon-all ground together.

Salt- ½ teaspoon or to taste

Cooking Oil-2 tablespoon

Method

Mash the *paneer* well.

Soak the bread pieces in water. Squeeze the water from the bread with both hands and then add to the mashed *paneer*.

Add all the other ingredients and mix well.

Shape the mashed *paneer* mixture into small flat patties.

In a shallow non-stick pan, heat the cooking oil and place the patties.

Brown the patties evenly on both sides and remove to a dish covered with an absorbent paper napkin.

Repeat till all the patties are cooked.

Serve hot with chutneys.

Prep time: 5 minutes

Cooking time: 3 minutes (Even if you are roasting more patties, each will still take 3 minutes to brown).

Total time: 8 minutes

Grilled *Paneer* or *Tofu*

Ingredients

Paneer (Indian Cottage cheese) or *Tofu*-200 grams (7oz) (1 cup)

Pizza/pasta sauce-1 tablespoon per piece

Salt- ½ teaspoon or to taste

Method

Slice the *paneer* (Indian cottage cheese) or *tofu* in such a way that they resemble half a slice of bread.

On each piece, sprinkle a little salt and cover it with a tablespoon of pizza/pasta sauce.

Marinate for 15 minutes.

Place the marinated pieces on a pre-heated grill and grill for about 5 minutes or till the *paneer* (Indian cottage cheese)/tofu becomes slightly cooked.

That's all.

Enjoy.

Prep time: 20 minutes for marinating and collecting all the ingredients together

Cooking time: 5 minutes

Total time: 25 minutes

Paneer Tikka (Cottage Cheese Patties)

Paneer Tikka is a great favourite that all restaurants from 5-star to wayside eateries in India serve with equal felicity.

Ingredients

Paneer- 500 grams (18oz) (2 cups) (cut into 2" cubes)

Yoghurt-200 grams (7oz) (1 cup)

Ginger-2 inches chopped finely

Garlic-6 cloves chopped finely

Tomato sauce/ketchup-2 tablespoon

Garam Masala-1/2 teaspoon

Tip: If you can't get ready-made *garam masala* mixture from a nearby Indian store, you can make yours by using 1 black cardamom, 3 green cardamoms, 4 cloves, and 1 inch cinnamon-all ground together for this dish.

Kashmiri Red Chilli powder–1/2 tea spoon (Recommended for colour, but if you like your dish to be really spicy, use some other hotter red chilli powder)

Salt- 1 teaspoon or to taste

Ghee (clarified butter) or butter (or any oil)-2 tablespoon

Method

In a bowl, beat together all the ingredients EXCEPT the *paneer* and the *ghee*.

Now add the *paneer* pieces and let them marinate for half an hour.

In a big non-stick pan, add the *ghee* and put it on your heat source.

Slowly add the *paneer* pieces along with the marinade.

Let all the water evaporate.

Gently turn the *paneer* pieces to give them a golden brown colour.

That's all. Your *Paneer Tikkas* are now ready.

If you wish, you can also put the *paneer* on a skewer and grill them to get the restaurant effect.

Prep time: 5 minutes (excluding the time to marinate)

Cooking time: 20 minutes

Total time: 30 minutes

Vegetable Kebabs

Have you ever seen those mouth-watering *Shami* Kebabs and wondered if they could have been prepared using vegetarian ingredients than mince chicken or mutton?

Don't worry I may have a solution.

Just use a clever mixture of lentils and legumes to prepare a similar looking Kebab.

Not only do these kebabs look similar but they can also deceive you in taste. This means that you will not be able to distinguish between a mince chicken/mutton kebab and a lentil-legume kebab.

Hara Bhara Kebab (Lush Green Kebab)

Ingredients

Peas-1 cup

Chana Dal (Split Chick Pea) -1/2 cup (soaked in water for at least 4 hours)

Chopped Garlic-4 cloves

Chopped Ginger-1 inch

Garam Masala (mixture of common Indian spices)-1/2 teaspoon

Tip: If you can't get ready-made *garam masala* mixture from a nearby Indian store, you can make yours by using 1 black cardamom, 3 green cardamoms, 4 cloves, and 1 inch cinnamon-all ground together for this dish.

Kashmiri Red Chilli powder–1/4 tea spoon (Recommended for colour, but if you like your dish to be really spicy, use some other hotter red chilli powder)

Salt- ½ teaspoon or to taste

Cooking Oil-2 tablespoon

Method

In a wok, add ½ tablespoon cooking oil and put it on your heat source.

As soon as the oil becomes warm, add the crushed garlic and ginger and roast for a minute.

Add the green peas and the soaked *chana* dal (split chick pea) without the water.

Stir well.

Now add the *garam masala*, red chilli powder and salt to taste.

Reduce the heat and cover the wok.

Cook till the split chick pea and peas become soft but not overcooked. Otherwise, you cannot make good kebabs.

Turn off the heat source and grind the mixture in a grinder.

Make small patties with this mixture and keep aside.

In a non-stick pan, add the left over cooking oil and put it on your heat source.

As soon as the oil becomes hot, add the patties and gently roast on both sides.

That's all. Your *Hara Bhara* Kebabs (Lush green Kebab) are ready.

Prep time: 5 minutes (in addition to the four hours required for soaking the split chick peas)

Cooking time: 15 minutes

Total time: 20 minutes

Spinach Kebab

Ingredients

Chopped Spinach-2 cups

Chana Dal (Split Chick Pea) -1/2 cup (soaked in water for at least 4 hours)

Chopped Garlic-4 cloves

Chopped Ginger-1 inch

Garam Masala (mixture of common Indian spices)-1/2 teaspoon

Tip: If you can't get ready-made *garam masala* mixture from a nearby Indian store, you can make yours by using 1 black cardamom, 3 green cardamoms, 4 cloves, and 1 inch cinnamon-all ground together for this dish.

Kashmiri Red Chilli powder–1/4 tea spoon (Recommended for colour, but if you like your dish to be really spicy, use some other hotter red chilli powder)

Salt- ½ teaspoon or to taste

Cooking Oil-2 tablespoon

Method

In a wok, add ½ tablespoon cooking oil and put it on your heat source.

As soon as the oil becomes warm, add the crushed garlic and ginger and roast for a minute.

Add the chopped spinach and the soaked *chana* dal (split chick pea) without the water.

Stir well.

Now add the *garam masala*, red chilli powder and salt to taste.

Reduce the heat and cover the wok.

Cook till the split chick pea and the spinach become soft but not overcooked. Otherwise, you cannot make good kebabs.

Turn off the heat source and grind the mixture in a grinder.

Make small patties with this mixture and keep aside.

In a non-stick pan, add the left over cooking oil and put it on your heat source.

As soon as the oil becomes hot, add the patties and gently roast on both sides.

That's all. Your Spinach Kebabs are ready.

Prep time: 5 minutes (in addition to the four hours required for soaking the split chick peas)

Cooking time: 15 minutes

Total time: 20 minutes

Soya Kebab

Ingredients

Soya granules-1 cup (soaked in water for 15 minutes)

Chana Dal (Split Chick Pea) -1/2 cup (soaked in water for at least 4 hours)

Chopped Garlic-4 cloves

Chopped Ginger-1 inch

Garam Masala (mixture of common Indian spices)-1/2 teaspoon

Tip: If you can't get ready-made *garam masala* mixture from a nearby Indian store, you can make yours by using 1 black cardamom, 3 green cardamoms, 4 cloves, and 1 inch cinnamon-all ground together for this dish.

Kashmiri Red Chilli powder–1/4 tea spoon (Recommended for colour, but if you like your dish to be really spicy, use some other hotter red chilli powder)

Salt- ½ teaspoon or to taste

Cooking Oil-2 tablespoon

Method

In a wok, add ½ tablespoon cooking oil and put it on your heat source.

As soon as the oil becomes warm, add the crushed garlic and ginger and roast for a minute.

Add the soya and the soaked *chana* dal (split chick pea) both without the water.

Stir well.

Now add the *garam masala*, red chilli powder and salt to taste.

Reduce the heat and cover the wok.

Cook till the split chick peas become soft but not overcooked. Otherwise, you cannot make good kebabs.

Turn off the heat source and grind the mixture in a grinder.

Make small patties with this mixture and keep aside.

In a non-stick pan, add the left over cooking oil and put it on your heat source.

As soon as the oil becomes hot, add the patties and gently roast on both sides.

That's all. Your Soya Kebabs are ready.

Prep time: 5 minutes (in addition to the four hours required for soaking the split chick peas)

Cooking time: 15 minutes

Total time: 20 minutes

Chutneys (Indian Home Made Sauces)

These are really mouth-watering sauces that can be made fresh, in smaller quantities without using any preservatives or other chemicals that the commercially made sauces come loaded with. These really go well with *pakoras* and *tikkis*.

Do, however, refrigerate these chutneys and try to use up within a week.

Tomato Chutney

Ingredients

Large ripe Tomatoes-5

Dates de-seeded-50 grams (2oz) (3 tablespoon)

Sugar-1 cup

Salt-1/2 teaspoon or to taste

Cumin seeds (*Jeera*)-1/2 teaspoon

Saunph (fennel seeds)-1/2 teaspoon

Mustard Oil (or your preferred oil)-1 teaspoon

Red dry chilli whole de-seeded (just for flavour and not to make it hot)-1

Method

In a wok, heat the oil and add the fennel, cumin seeds and the red chilli.

As soon as the mixture starts crackling (which takes only a few seconds), add the tomatoes.

Please make sure that the mixture doesn't burn otherwise your chutney will taste awful!!!

Stir the tomatoes well and add the sugar and salt.

When the tomatoes are almost done, add the dates and cook for a few minutes more.

If the chutney becomes too thick, you may add a little water but this is not necessary.

That's all. Your delicious tomato chutney with dates is ready.

Have it with *pakoras*, *tikkis* or even with your full Indian meal platter, as I like it.

Prep time: 5 minutes

Cooking time: 10 minutes

Total time: 15 minutes

Dhania Pudina Chutney (Coriander Mint Chutney)–Sweet Version

This is the JIFFIEST sauce on earth as it is prepared without cooking anything. All the natural vitamins and anti-oxidants, therefore, are fully preserved which makes this quite a nutritious chutney.

Ingredients

Green Mint (*Pudina*) Leaves-100 grams (3.5oz) (half cup)

Green Coriander (*Dhania*) Leaves-100 grams (3.5oz) (half cup)

Whole De-seeded Green Chilli-1

Tamarind (*Imli*) made into paste-50 grams (2oz) (3 tablespoon)

Sugar-4 tablespoon

Salt-1/2 teaspoon or to taste

Crushed cumin seeds (*Jeera*)-1/2 teaspoon

Method

Grind together all the ingredients in a grinder.

Take the mixture out in a bowl and taste to see if the sugar and salt is to your liking.

That's all.

Your *Dhania Pudina* chutney is ready, to be eaten with any snack or main dish.

Prep time: 5 minutes

Cooking time: Nil

Total time: 5 minutes

Dhania Pudina Chutney (Coriander Mint Chutney)–Salty Version

Ingredients

Green Mint (*Pudina*) Leaves-100 grams (3.50z) (half cup)

Green Coriander (*Dhania*) Leaves-100 grams (3.50z) (half cup)

Whole De-seeded Green Chilli-1

Lemon juice-2 tablespoon

Salt-1/2 teaspoon or to taste

Method

Grind together all the ingredients in a grinder.

Take the mixture out in a bowl and taste to see if the salt is to your liking.

That's all.

Your *Dhania Pudina* chutney is ready, to be eaten with any snack or main dish.

Prep time: 5 minutes

Cooking time: Nil

Total time: 5 minutes

Raita

Raitas are yoghurt based dishes that are served with the main meal in Northern India. You take a spoonful of this once in a while basically to cleanse your palate.

Again, you don't have to cook anything!

Cucumber *Raita*

Ingredients

Yoghurt-400 grams (14oz) (1 + 1/2 cups)

Cucumber-1 cut into bite size pieces

Cumin (*Jeera*) seeds (pre-roasted and crushed)-1 teaspoon

Salt-1 teaspoon or to taste

Sugar-2 teaspoon

Method

In a bowl, whisk the yoghurt well with salt, sugar and the roasted cumin seeds. Add then the cucumber pieces. That's all.

Your Cucumber *Raita* is ready.

Prep time: 5 minutes

Cooking time: Nil

Total time: 5 minutes

Raita with Mint and Coriander Leaves

Ingredients

Yoghurt-400 grams (14oz) (1 + 1/2 cups)

Chopped Mint (*Pudina*) leaves-20 grams (1oz) (1 tablespoon)

Chopped Coriander (*Dhania*) leaves-20 grams (1oz) (1 tablespoon)

Chaat Masala-1/2 teaspoon

You should be able to get *Chaat Masala* from any Indian store. However, if you can't, you can make it at home by mixing together 1 teaspoon dried mango powder + 1 teaspoon rock salt + 1 teaspoon cumin powder + ½ teaspoon asafoetida + ½ teaspoon chilli powder.

Black Salt-1/4 teaspoon

Cumin (*Jeera*) pre-roasted and crushed-1 teaspoon

Salt-1 teaspoon or to taste

Sugar-4 teaspoon

Method

In a bowl, whisk the yoghurt well with all ingredients EXCEPT THE CHOPPED MINT AND CORIANDER LEAVES.

Now add the leaves.

That's all.

Your *Raita* with Mint and Coriander Leaves is ready.

Prep time: 5 minutes

Cooking time: Nil

Total time: 5 minutes

Lauki **(Bottle Gourd)** *Raita*

Ingredients

Yoghurt-400 grams (14oz) (1 + 1/2 cups)

Lauki (bottle gourd)- 250 grams -1 cup (peeled and grated)

Mustard Oil- 1 tablespoon (for that special flavour)

Cumin (*Jeera*) seeds (pre-roasted and crushed)-1 teaspoon

Salt-1 teaspoon or to taste

Sugar-1 teaspoon

Water- 1 cup (for boiling the bottle gourd)

Method

Place a vessel with water on your heat source. When the water starts boiling, add the grated bottle gourd, and let it boil for 2 minutes. Strain and keep aside. In a bowl, whisk the yoghurt well with salt, sugar, mustard oil and the roasted cumin seeds.

Now add the boiled bottle gourd. Mix well. That's all. Your *Lauki Raita* is ready.

Prep time: 5 minutes

Cooking time: 5 minutes

Total time: 10 minutes

Chapter 2: Dry Veggie Dishes

"*Many people are turned off at eating vegetarian because of the misconception that all dishes are just an arrangement of bland vegetables.*"

–Marcus Samuelsson

Indians have dry veggies dishes regardless of whether they already have a curry on their meal platter (*Thali*) or not. In fact, it is almost compulsory to have a curry balanced by a dry dish.

For non-Indians, we suggest that you try a curry dish if you are having rice on the side, and a dry dish if you are having any kind of bread.

But what the heck. Feel free to break all rules and do what your heart pleases.

In that backdrop, we present here 24 outstanding dry veggie dishes from all over India. Eastern Indian cuisine dominates with as many as 11 dishes. But there are 7 North Indian dishes and 3 each from West and South India.

Beans with Coconut

This is a great South Indian dish infused with the additional thyroid improving goodness of coconut.

Serves 3-4

Ingredients

French beans-400 grams (14oz) (1 + 1/2 cups)

Grated fresh (preferred) coconut-1

Chopped up Ginger-2 inches

Black Mustard Whole (*Rai*) -1/2 teaspoon

Curry leaves-10

Cooking Oil-1 tablespoon

Salt to taste

Method

Wash the French beans thoroughly and cut them into one inch pieces.

Steam the beans (for example, in a rice cooker or microwave steamer) for 5 minutes.

This is to help reduce calories.

In a pan, add the cooking oil and put it on your heat source.

As soon as the oil warms up, add the black mustard and curry leaves.

As the mustard splutters, add the ginger.

Stir for a minute.

Add the French beans, salt and the grated fresh coconut.

Mix and stir well.

That's all. Your simple South-Indian Beans with Coconut veggie dish is ready.

Prep time: 5 minutes

Cooking time: 8 minutes

Total time: 13 minutes

Cabbage, Carrot and Peas with Coconut

A wonderful medley of delicious veggie recipe from South India.

Serves 3-4

Ingredients

Cabbage-400 grams (14oz) (1 + 1/2 cups)

Carrot-100 grams (3.5oz) (half cup)

Peas shelled-100 grams (3.5oz) (half cup)

Grated fresh (preferred) coconut-1

Chopped up Ginger-2 inches

Black Mustard Whole (*Rai*) -1/2 teaspoon

Curry leaves-10

Cooking Oil-1 tablespoon

Salt to taste

Method

Wash the Cabbage and Carrots thoroughly and cut them into one inch pieces.

Steam the cabbage, carrot and peas (for example, in a rice cooker or microwave steamer) for 5 minutes.

This is to help reduce calories.

In a pan, add the cooking oil and put it on your heat source.

As soon as the oil warms up, add the black mustard and curry leaves.

As the mustard splutters, add the ginger.

Stir for a minute.

Add the steamed vegetables, salt and the grated fresh coconut.

Mix and stir well.

That's all. Your delicious Cabbage, Carrot and Peas with Coconut medley is ready.

Prep time: 5 minutes

Cooking time: 10 minutes

Total time: 15 minutes

Bhhindi (Okra) Fry

This is how the East Indians tame this sticky vegetable. You can add a potato or two, if you so wish, for variety.

Serves 3-4

Ingredients

Bhhindi (Okra)–500 grams (18oz) (2 cups) (washed and cut into ½ inch cubes, breadth wise)

Cumin (*Jeera*) Seeds- 1 teaspoon

Dry red chilli- 1 (whole)

Onion – 1 (chopped)

Cooking oil- 3 tablespoon

Salt- ½ teaspoon or to taste

Method

Place a wok (or deep sauce pan) on your heat source.

Add the cooking oil.

When the oil heats up, add the cumin seeds and the dry red chilli (whole).

As soon as the cumin seeds turn brown, add the okra and stir well.

When the okra starts turning light brown, add the onion and the salt.

Stir well till the onions turn translucent.

Switch off the heat source.

With a slotted spoon, remove the veggies onto a plate lined with a paper napkin to help absorb the excess oil.

That's all. Your simple Okra Fry is ready.

Prep time: 5 minutes

Cooking time: 10 minutes

Total time: Approximately 15 minutes

Bhhindi Kurkure **(Okra Crispy Fried)**

This is a great party dish, North-Indian style, when you couldn't be bothered about calories.

But if you are, we present the air fryer version as well.

Serves 3-4

Ingredients

Bhhindi (Okra)- 500 grams (18oz) (2 cups) (washed and slit into half)

Cumin (*Jeera*) Seeds- 1 teaspoon

Red chilli powder- ½ teaspoon

Turmeric (*Haldi*) powder- ½ teaspoon

Chick pea flour (*Besan*)-1 tablespoon

Coriander (*Dhania)* powder-1 teaspoon

Salt- ½ teaspoon or to taste

Cooking oil- Enough to deep fry (unless you decide to use an air fryer, in which case just one teaspoon of cooking oil would be needed)

Method using a wok/deep sauce pan

Except the cooking oil, add all the ingredients to the slit okra and set aside for 15 minutes. This will help the flavours seep in.

Place a wok (or deep sauce pan) on your heat source.

Add enough cooking oil to help deep fry the okra.

When the oil heats up, add two tablespoon full of okra mixture.

Gently fry till the okra acquires a golden colour.

With a slotted spoon, remove the okra onto a plate lined with a paper napkin to help absorb the excess oil.

Repeat till all the okra is fried.

That's all. Your Crispy Okra fry is ready.

Method using an air fryer

Except the cooking oil, add all the ingredients to the slit okra and set aside for 15 minutes. This will help the flavours seep in.

Pre-heat the air fryer at 200 degree C (392 degrees F) for 5 minutes. With a silicon brush, gently brush the bottom grill with a little oil. Place all the okra mixture together in the air fryer.

Fry for 12 minutes at 200 degree C (392 degrees F). That's all. Your Crispy Okra fry is ready.

Prep time: 5 minutes (excluding marinating time) for wok/ pan; plus 5 minutes if using the air fryer

Cooking time: 10 minutes @2 minutes per batch for wok/pan; 12 minutes for air fryer

Total time: Approximately 15 minutes for wok/pan; 22 minutes for air fryer

Palak Baingan (Spinach-Aubergine)

Serves 3-4

This is a true blood Eastern India dish using *pachphoran*. You master this and you can then cook any other *pachphoran* recipe with élan.

Ingredients

Spinach (*Palak*)–1 Kg or 2lb or 4 cups (washed and chopped)

Aubergines (*Baingan*)-1 (roughly 200 grams or 7oz or 1 cup) (washed and cut into 1" cubes)

Onion Medium—1 (chopped)

Tomatoes--2 (washed and chopped)

Pachphoran, which is a mixture of *Jeera* (cumin), *Saunf* (fennel seeds), *Methi* seeds (fenugreek seeds), *Rai* (black mustard seeds), and *Kalonji* (onion seeds) in equal proportion–1 teaspoon

Cooking oil (preferably Mustard)–1 tablespoon full

Salt-1/2 teaspoon (or to taste)

Method using a pressure cooker

Heat oil in a pressure cooker and add the *pachphoran*.

As the *pachphoran* begins to splutter (which takes a few seconds), add the chopped onions and sauté on low flame for a minute.

Add the washed and chopped spinach, aubergine and the tomatoes. Stir the same to evenly mix it.

Close the lid of the cooker with the weight and let it come to full pressure.

Immediately remove the pressure cooker from your heat source, cool it under running cold water and release the pressure.

Now open the lid and put the cooker back on fire. This is because Spinach gives out a lot of water. So let it dry up somewhat before you serve.

At this juncture add the salt and mix well.

That's all. Your delicious *Palak Baingan* is ready.

Method using a wok/deep sauce pan

Heat oil in a wok/deep sauce pan and add the *pachphoran*.

As the *pachphoran* begins to splutter (which takes a few seconds), add the chopped onions and sauté on low flame for a minute.

Add the washed and chopped spinach, aubergine and the tomatoes. Stir the same to evenly mix it.

Cover the wok/deep pan with a lid and reduce the heat to minimum.

Since spinach leaves a lot of water, you don't need to add any additional water like you do with other vegetables. Let the vegetables cook to your liking for about 10 minutes.

At this juncture add the salt and mix well.

Let the veggies dry up somewhat before you serve.

That's all. Your delicious *Palak Baingan* is ready.

Prep time: 5 minutes

Cooking time: 10 minutes with a pressure cooker, 15 minutes with a wok/deep pan

Total time: 15 minutes with a pressure cooker, 20 minutes with a wok/deep pan

Lauki Plain (Bottle Gourd)

This is the easiest way to cook *Lauki* the Eastern Indian way, with absolutely the minimum of spices. So no turmeric, no *garam masala* or *pachphoran*. Nothing can be simpler and still be so tasty.

Serves 3-4

Ingredients

Lauki (Bottle Gourd)–1 (roughly a kg or 2lb or 4 cups); peel and cut into bite size pieces

Onion Medium—1 (chopped)

Jeera (Cumin)–1/2 teaspoon

Dry Red Whole (not powder) Chilli–1 (Just for flavour and not to make the food spicy)

Salt–1 level teaspoon (or to taste)

Cooking oil–1 tablespoon

Method using a pressure cooker

In a pressure cooker, add the cooking oil and when it warms up, add the cumin seeds (*jeera*) and the dry red whole chilli.

As soon as the cumin (*jeera*) starts browning, add the chopped onion and sauté it till these become translucent.

Add the *lauki* (gourd) pieces, and the salt. Stir well.

Close the pressure cooker's lid with weight and let it come to full pressure.

Immediately remove the pressure cooker from your heat source, cool it under running cold water and release the pressure.

Now open the lid and put the cooker back on fire. This is because the bottle gourd (*lauki*) gives out a lot of water. So let it dry up somewhat before you serve.

That's all. Your *Lauki* Plain is ready to be served.

Method using a wok/deep sauce pan

In a wok/deep sauce pan, add the cooking oil and when it warms up, add the cumin seeds (*jeera*) and the dry red whole chilli.

As soon as the cumin (*jeera*) starts browning, add the chopped onion and sauté it till these become translucent.

Add the *lauki* (gourd) pieces, and the salt. Stir well.

Cover the wok/deep pan with a lid and reduce the heat to minimum.

Since gourd leaves a lot of water, you don't need to add any additional water like you do with other vegetables. Let the gourd cook to your liking for about 10 minutes.

You may poke it once in a while with a fork to see whether the gourd has been cooked well.

Let the dish dry up somewhat before you serve.

That's all. Your *Lauki* Plain is ready to be served.

Prep time: 5 minutes

Cooking time: 10 minutes with a pressure cooker; 15 minutes with a wok/pan

Total time: 15 minutes with a pressure cooker, 20 minutes with a wok/pan

Gobi Masala **Full (Full Cauliflower Spicy)**

This is a gourmet North Indian dish. Your cauliflower will never look this beautiful, I promise.

Serves 3-4

Ingredients

Cauliflower -1 (full)

Onion-1 (chopped)

Garlic-2 cloves

Ginger-1/2 inch

Cumin (*Jeera*) seeds- 1 teaspoon

Turmeric (*Haldi*) powder-1/2 teaspoon

Coriander (*Dhania*) powder- 1 teaspoon

Garam Masala (mixture of common Indian spices) crushed- 1/2 tea spoon

Tip: If you can't get ready-made *garam masala* mixture from a nearby Indian store, you can make yours by using 1 black cardamom, 3 green cardamoms, 4 cloves, and 1 inch cinnamon-all ground together.

Kashmiri Red Chilli powder–1/2 tea spoon (Recommended for colour, but if you like your dish to

be really spicy, use some other hotter red chilli powder)

Tomato puree-1 cup (200 grams)

Salt-1 tea spoon (or to taste)

Sugar- ½ teaspoon

Cooking Oil-3 table spoon

Water- ½ cup

Method

Wash the cauliflower well and steam it (for example, in a rice cooker or microwave steamer) for 10 minutes.

Meanwhile, chop the onion, garlic, and ginger and blend it into a paste.

After the cauliflower is steamed, place a wok on your heat source and pour in the oil.

When the oil heats up, place the steamed cauliflower upside down (with the florets side dipped in the oil).

As soon as the floret side becomes golden, remove the cauliflower from the wok and keep aside.

Now add the cumin seeds to the oil.

As soon as the cumin seeds turn brown, which takes just a few seconds (do please make sure they don't burn), add the onion, garlic and ginger paste.

Sauté well till the paste starts giving a nice aroma.

Now add the chilli powder, turmeric powder, *garam masala*, coriander powder, salt and sugar.

Sauté till the mixture turns a light brown colour.

To this mixture, now add the tomato puree.

Stir till the mixture dries up somewhat.

Add the water and place the cauliflower in the wok upside down with the florets dipped in the mixture.

Let this all cook together for about 5 minutes.

Remove to a serving dish, with the florets side now facing up.

Pour all the mixture from the wok over the cauliflower.

That's all. Your whole *gobi masala* is ready.

Prep time: 10 minutes

Cooking time: 30 minutes

Total time: 40 minutes

Aloo Gobi (Potato-Cauliflower)

This is a very popular North Indian dry veggie dish. Alone, it goes well with *pooris* (fried non leavened Indian bread). Otherwise, it can be paired with another curry dish and/or lentil dish and enjoyed with rice or *rotis*.

Serves 3-4

Ingredients

Potatoes-2

Cauliflower-1

Onion-1

Garlic-2

Ginger-1/2 inch

Turmeric (*Haldi*)-1/2 tea spoon

Garam Masala (mixture of common Indian spices) crushed- 1/2 tea spoon

Tip: If you can't get ready-made *garam masala* mixture from a nearby Indian store, you can make yours by using 1 black cardamom, 3 green cardamoms, 4 cloves, and 1 inch cinnamon-all ground together.

Kashmiri Red Chilli powder–1/4 tea spoon (Recommended for colour, but if you like your dish to

be really spicy, use some other hotter red chilli powder)

Tomato-1

Salt-1 level tea spoon (or to taste)

Cooking Oil-1 table spoon

Method

Cut the potatoes into small pieces and also separate the florets of the cauliflower.

Steam this (for example, in a rice cooker or microwave steamer) for 5 minutes.

Meanwhile, chop the onion, garlic, ginger and tomatoes.

In a wok, heat the oil, and add the chopped onion, garlic and ginger.

When this mixture starts becoming translucent, add the tomatoes and let the tomatoes cook.

Add the steamed vegetables to this and sprinkle *haldi, garam masala*, chilli powder and salt.

Let this all cook together for about 3 minutes. A table spoon or two of water helps in blending all together.

That's all. Your dry *aloo gobi* is ready.

Note: Please note that if you don't steam the veggies first, you can proceed as above but you will then need triple the quantity of oil and will need to cook the vegetables for at least 15 minutes.

Prep time: 5 minutes

Cooking time: 15 minutes

Total time: 20 minutes

Mashed Potato Southern Indian Style

This recipe goes well as an accompaniment to various Southern Indian rice dishes.

Serves 3-4

Ingredients

Potatoes-1/2 kg (18oz) (2 cups)

Sliced Onion-1

Turmeric (*Haldi*) powder-1/2 teaspoon

Black Mustard (*Rai*)-1/2 teaspoon

Curry leaves-a few

Tamarind *(Imli)* paste-1 tablespoon dissolved in 1/2 cup water

Cooking Oil-1 tablespoon

Salt- 1 level teaspoon (or to taste)

Whole Green chillies (just for flavour and not to make it hot)-1

Grated fresh (preferred) coconut-3 tablespoon

Method

Boil and peel the potatoes and then mash them with a fork.

In a wok, put the cooking oil and put it on your heat source.

As soon as the oil warms up, add the mustard, the onions and the whole green chilli.

Sauté till the onions become translucent.

Then add the turmeric, the curry leaves, the grated coconut and the salt.

Sauté for a few more minutes.

Now, add the mashed potatoes and mix well.

Add the tamarind paste. This will impart a certain tartness to the potatoes and also help in mixing up all the ingredients together.

Let the mixture dry up somewhat which should hardly take a minute or two. Now, turn off the heat source and take out the mashed potatoes in a serving bowl.

That's all. Your mashed potato South Indian style is ready.

Prep time: 5 minutes

Cooking time: 5 minutes (if potatoes are already boiled), otherwise please include the time for boiling the potatoes.

Total time: 10 minutes

Aloo Bharta (Mashed Potato)

This typically Eastern India, or rather Bihari, dish is a must with Khichdi. I give a milder version here. But if you need to spice it up, then mix some stuffed red chilli pickles to this and enjoy.

Serves 3-4

Ingredients

Potatoes-1/2 kg (18oz) (2 cups)

Onion-1 (chopped finely)

Green chilli de-seeded (for flavour)-1 (Retain the seeds if you like it hot)

Fresh Coriander (*Dhania*) leaves-50 grams (2oz) (3 tablespoon)

Mustard oil (if you want the authentic flavour)-1/2 teaspoon

Salt-to taste

Method

Boil and peel the potatoes, then mash them well.

Add the salt and the mustard oil.

Add the onion, chillies and coriander (all raw).

Mix well.

That's all. Your Bihari *Aloo Bharta* is ready.

Prep time: Approx. 15 minutes.

Only the time taken to boil and peel the potatoes and to chop onions, etc.

Cooking time: No cooking time

Total time: 15 minutes maximum

Kohra Bari (Yellow Pumpkin with Spicy Lentil Dumplings)

This is a true blood Eastern India dish using *pachphoran*. You master this and you can then cook any other *pachphoran* recipe with élan.

Ingredients

Kohra (Yellow pumpkin)–1 Kg or 2lb or 4 cups (washed and chopped with the skin removed)

Aubergines (*Baingan*)-1 (roughly 200 grams or 7oz or 1 cup) (washed and cut into 1" cubes)

Cauliflower stem (not the florets) - 2-3 pieces (chopped)

Tomatoes–2 (washed and chopped)

Urad Bari (Black lentil spicy dumpling) – 2 (150 grams approx.), broken in to bite size pieces

Pachphoran, which is a mixture of *Jeera* (cumin), *Saunf* (fennel seeds), *Methi* seeds (fenugreek seeds), *Rai* (black mustard seeds), and *Kalonji* (onion seeds) in equal proportion–1 teaspoon

Red Chilli (dry) - 1 whole

Cooking oil (preferably Mustard)–1 tablespoon full

Salt-1 teaspoon (or to taste)

Sugar- 1 teaspoon

Method using a pressure cooker

Heat oil in a pressure cooker and add the *pachphoran* and the red chilli (whole).

As the *pachphoran* begins to splutter (which takes a few seconds), add the *urad baris* and sauté on low flame for 1/2 a minute.

Add the washed and chopped yellow pumpkin, aubergine, cauliflower stems and the tomatoes.

Stir well to evenly mix it all.

Add the sugar and the salt.

Close the lid of the cooker with the weight and let it come to full pressure.

Reduce the heat to minimum (SIM on a gas stove) and cook for 5 minutes more.

Remove the pressure cooker from your heat source, and let it cool down.

Now open the lid and put the cooker back on fire. This is because pumpkin gives out a lot of water. So let it dry up somewhat before you serve.

That's all. Your exotic *Kohra Bari* dish is ready to be served.

Method using a wok/deep sauce pan

Heat oil in a wok/deep sauce pan and add the *pachphoran* and the red chilli (whole).

As the *pachphoran* begins to splutter (which takes a few seconds), add the *urad baris* and sauté on low flame for 1/2 a minute.

Add the washed and chopped yellow pumpkin, aubergine, cauliflower stems and the tomatoes.

Stir well to evenly mix it all.

Add the sugar and the salt.

Cover the wok/deep pan with a lid and reduce the heat to minimum.

Since pumpkin leaves a lot of water, you don't need to add any additional water like you do with other vegetables. Let the dish cook to your liking for about 10 minutes. Let it also dry up somewhat before you serve.

That's all. Your exotic *Kohra Bari* dish is ready to be served.

Prep time: 10 minutes

Cooking time: 10 minutes with a pressure cooker, 15 minutes with a wok/deep pan

Total time: 15 minutes with a pressure cooker, 20 minutes with a wok/deep pan

Meetha Kohra (Plain Pumpkin Delight-Sweet)

This Eastern Indian veggie is sweet, both literally and figuratively. Try this with *pooris* or *parathas* and I'm sure you will agree with me that ripe pumpkin made any other way can't taste so delicious.

Serves 3-4

Ingredients

Ripe yellow pumpkin-1 Kg (2lb) (4 cups)

Fenugreek seeds (*Methi*)-1/2 teaspoon

Coriander (*Dhania*) powder- 2 heap teaspoon

Turmeric (*Haldi*) powder-1 teaspoon

Kashmiri Red Chilli powder–1/2 tea spoon (Recommended for colour, but if you like your dish to be really spicy, use some other hotter red chilli powder)

Mango Dry powder (*Amchoor*)-1/2 teaspoon

Asafoetida powder (*Hing*)-1 level teaspoon

Cooking Oil-2 tablespoon

Water-1 cup

Sugar-3 teaspoon

Salt-1 teaspoon (or to taste)

Method using a pressure cooker

Peel the pumpkin and cut into bite size pieces.

Place a pressure cooker on the heat source and add the cooking oil.

When the cooking oil warms up, add the Fenugreek seeds (*Methi*) and thereafter add the pumpkins.

REMEMBER FENUGREEK SEEDS (METHI) BURN VERY FAST, SO DON'T LEAVE IT IN THE OIL WITHOUT THE PUMPKIN FOR MORE THAN A FEW SECONDS.

Now, add all the other ingredients.

Stir well for approximately 2 minutes to ensure that all the ingredients are well blended and very lightly fried.

Pour the water over the pumpkin and close the lid with weight.

Let the cooker come to full pressure.

Reduce the heat and let the cooker remain on minimum heat for 5 minutes.

Thereafter turn off the heat source and let the cooker cool on its own.

Open the lid and place the cooker back on the heat source without the lid.

Dry the pumpkin, that is, let the water evaporate till you have a nice thick consistency.

That's all. Your delicious *Meetha Kohra* pumpkin dish is ready.

Method using a wok/deep sauce pan

Peel the pumpkin and cut into bite size pieces.

Place a wok/deep sauce pan on the heat source and add the cooking oil.

When the cooking oil warms up, add the Fenugreek seeds (*Methi*) and thereafter add the pumpkins.

REMEMBER FENUGREEK SEEDS (*METHI*) BURN VERY FAST, SO DON'T LEAVE IT IN THE OIL WITHOUT THE PUMPKIN FOR MORE THAN A FEW SECONDS.

Now, add all the other ingredients.

Stir well for approximately 2 minutes to ensure that all the ingredients are well blended and very lightly fried.

Pour the water over the pumpkin and cover the wok/deep pan with a lid and reduce the heat to minimum.

Let the pumpkin cook to your liking for about 15 minutes.

Dry the pumpkin, that is, let the water evaporate till you have a nice thick consistency.

That's all. Your delicious *Meetha Kohra* pumpkin dish is ready.

Prep time: 8 minutes

Cooking time: 15 minutes with a pressure cooker; 30 minutes with a wok/deep pan

Total time: 23 minutes with a pressure cooker; 38 minutes with a wok/deep pan

---

Chhola **Dry (Whole Chick Pea Dry)**

This is an excellent dish which can be had even as a mid-morning or afternoon snack. It is healthy as it is prepared without using even a drop of oil.

Serves 3-4

Ingredients

Whole white chick pea (Kabuli *Chana* or *Chhola*)-1 small cup

Onions-1 (chopped)

Tomatoes-2 (chopped)

Fresh Coriander leaves- 1 tea spoon (chopped)

Deseeded green chilli- 1 (optional) (chopped)

Fresh Lemon juice- 1 table spoon

Salt: ½ teaspoon or to taste

Method

Soak the chick pea in a vessel with water (which covers the chick peas completely) at least for 4 hours. This way when you cook the chick peas, they become nice and tender and take less time to cook.

Put the pre-soaked chick peas in a pressure cooker, with enough water to cover the chick peas.

Switch on the heat source and close the lid of the pressure cooker with weight.

When the cooker comes to full pressure, i.e. when steam starts escaping from the vent (don't worry, you will hear that typical sound), reduce the heat (to Sim on a gas stove) and let the chick peas cook for 10 minutes more.

Turn off the heat source and let the cooker cool down.

Take out the chickpeas (without the water) into a serving bowl.

Add the chopped onion, tomatoes, coriander leaves, green chilli, salt and lemon juice and mix well.

That's all. Your delicious dry *chhola* is ready.

Prep time: Soak overnight or at least for 4 hours. After that prep time should be 5 minutes for washing and collecting all ingredients.

Cooking time: 15 minutes with pressure cooker

Total time: 20 minutes (without the pre-soak time)

Parwal Aloo Bhujia (Pointed Gourd and Potato Dry)

In season, this is the favourite dish of Biharis in Eastern India. So if you can hold of some *parwal*, you should be able to rustle up this simple dish without any problems.

Serves 3-4

Ingredients

Potatoes-2

Parwal- 400 grams (14oz) (1 + 1/2 cups)

Onion-1 (large, chopped)

Turmeric (*Haldi*) powder-1/2 tea spoon

Tomato-1 (chopped)

Salt-1/2 tea spoon (or to taste)

Cooking Oil- 2 table spoon

Method

Cut the potatoes into small pieces.

Scratch (not peel) the surface of the *parwals* and wash well.

Now slit each *parwal* into 4 long slices.

In a wok, heat the oil, and add the potato.

Stir till the potatoes are a little cooked.

Now add the slit *parwals*.

Fry till the *parwals* and potatoes are almost done, in about 10 minutes.

Now add the chopped onion, salt and turmeric powder.

When the onions turn translucent, add the tomatoes and let the tomatoes cook.

Let this all cook together for about 3 minutes.

That's all. Your dry *aloo parwal* is ready.

Prep time: 10 minutes

Cooking time: 20 minutes

Total time: 30 minutes

Parwal Bharwan (Pointed Gourd Stuffed)

Again from Bihar (Eastern India), this is a gourmet dish. Do try it when you wish to lift the humble *parwal* to something sublime.

Serves 3-4

Ingredients

Parwal- 500 grams (1/2 Kg or 18oz or 2 cups)

Onion-2 (large, chopped)

Ginger- 1 inch chopped

Garlic- 6 cloves chopped

Turmeric (*Haldi*) powder-1/2 tea spoon

Coriander (*Dhania*) powder- 1 teaspoon

Cumin (*Jeera*) seeds- 1 teaspoon

Garam Masala (mixture of common Indian spices) crushed- 1/2 tea spoon

Tip: If you can't get ready-made *garam masala* mixture from a nearby Indian store, you can make yours by using 1 black cardamom, 3 green cardamoms, 4 cloves, and 1 inch cinnamon-all ground together.

Kashmiri Red Chilli powder–1/4 tea spoon (Recommended for colour, but if you like your dish to

be really spicy, use some other hotter red chilli powder)

Tomato-1 (chopped)

Salt-1/2 tea spoon (or to taste)

Sugar- ¼ teaspoon

Cooking Oil- 3 table spoon

Thread- enough for tying each *parwal* separately.

Method

Scratch (not peel) the surface of the *parwals* and wash well.

Now slit each *parwal* lengthwise and take out all the seeds and flesh leaving behind just a hollowed shell.

In a wok, add 1 tablespoon oil, and place it on your heat source.

As the oil heats up, add the cumin seeds.

As soon as the cumin seeds turn brown, which takes just a few seconds (do please make sure they don't burn), add the chopped onion, garlic and ginger.

Sauté well till the onions become translucent and start emitting a nice aroma.

Add the scooped out flesh of the *parwal* along with the chilli powder, turmeric powder, *garam masala*, coriander powder, salt and sugar.

Sauté till the mixture turns a light brown colour.

To this mixture, now add the tomatoes.

Roast well till the tomatoes are cooked and the mixture dries up.

Switch off the heat source and let the mixture cool down.

As soon as you can touch the mixture, fill up about a tablespoon of mixture into each hollowed *parwal*.

Tie with a thread to secure the mixture inside.

Take another wok and pour in the remaining two tablespoon of cooking oil.

As the oil heats up, add the stuffed *parwal* and gently fry till done, in about 10 minutes.

That's all. Your *parwal bharwan* is ready.

Do please remember to remove the thread before serving.

Prep time: 10 minutes

Cooking time: 25 minutes

Total time: 35 minutes

Paneer Dopyaza (Cottage Cheese with Onions)

This is the classic North Indian dish that you will find everywhere, in homes, *dhabas* as well as fancy restaurants.

Serves 3-4

Ingredients

Paneer (Cottage cheese)–1/2 Kg (500 grams or 18oz or 2 cups)

Onion-1 large (chopped)

Ginger-2 inch piece

Garlic-8 Cloves

Tomatoes-3 (chopped)

(Onion + Ginger + Garlic + Tomatoes blended into a fine paste)

Onion- 2 large (chopped) separately for frying

Garam Masala-1/2 teaspoon

Tip: If you can't get ready-made *garam masala* mixture from a nearby Indian store, you can make yours by using 1 black cardamom, 3 green cardamoms, 4 cloves, and 1 inch cinnamon-all ground together for this dish.

Salt–1 teaspoon (or to taste)

Turmeric (*Haldi*) powder–1 and 1/2 teaspoon (1 teaspoon for marinating the *paneer* and half for the curry).

Kashmiri Red Chilli powder–1/4 tea spoon (Recommended for colour, but if you like your dish to be really spicy, use some other hotter red chilli powder)

Fresh green chillies whole–4 (Whole chillies impart a lovely flavour to the cuisine and will NOT make it spicy)

Cooking oil–2 tablespoon

Water-1/2 cup (roughly 125 ml)

Vessels: One non-stick frying pan and one *kadai* (wok)

Method

Take the *paneer* (cottage cheese) and dry roast it on a non- stick pan till it turns a golden brown. It can then be cut into bite size pieces.

(Most recipes would advise that you fry these pieces in oil, which you can try if you don't mind the additional calories!)

In a wok, add the oil and put the wok on your heat source.

As the oil heats up, add the chopped onions and fry till they turn golden.

Remove from the wok and keep aside.

Now put the onion+ garlic + ginger+ tomato paste in the wok and stir well.

Add the salt, *garam masala*, turmeric and red chilli powder.

Keep on stirring till the paste is well fried and you can see some oil glistening on the sides of the wok.

Now add the roasted *paneer* and stir well.

Add ½ cup of water and let the water come to a boil.

Now add the whole fresh green chillies and the fried onions.

Reduce the heat to the minimum (SIM on a gas stove) and cook for 5 more minutes.

That's all. Your *Paneer Do Pyaza* (Cottage Cheese with fried onions) is ready.

Prep time: 10 minutes

Cooking time: 15 minutes

Total time: 25 minutes

Potato with Spring Onions

This is a simple dish from Eastern India that infuses the goodness of spring onions in to the humble potato. And the flavours are NOT Chinese!

Serves 3-4

Ingredients

Potatoes- 400 grams or 2 cups (boiled, peeled and cut in to bite size pieces)

Spring Onion-250 grams (9oz) (1 cup) (chopped along with the green stems)

Coriander (*Dhania*) powder- 1 teaspoon

Kashmiri Red Chilli powder–1/4 tea spoon (Recommended for colour, but if you like your dish to be really spicy, use some other hotter red chilli powder)

Cumin (*Jeera*) seeds- 1 teaspoon

Salt-1 tea spoon (or to taste)

Cooking Oil- 2 table spoon

Method

In a wok, pour the cooking oil, and place it on your heat source.

As the oil heats up, add the cumin seeds.

As soon as the cumin seeds turn brown, which takes just a few seconds (do please make sure they don't burn), add the chopped potatoes.

Stir till the potatoes start turning a golden brown in colour.

Now add the red chilli, coriander powder and the salt.

Stir well.

Now add the spring onions and let this all cook together for about a minute.

That's all. Your Potato with spring onion dish is ready.

Prep time: 15 minutes (including for boiling the potatoes)

Cooking time: 10 minutes

Total time: 25 minutes

Aloo Methi (Potato with Fenugreek leaves)

Another classic Bihari (Eastern Indian) dish that harnesses the diabetes fighting properties of *methi* (fenugreek) in a very appetising a manner.

Serves 3-4

Ingredients

Potatoes- 400 grams or 2 cups (boiled, peeled and cut in to bite size pieces)

Fenugreek leaves-400 grams or 2 cups (pluck only the leaves, and leave out the stems) Blanch these (i.e. put these in boiling water for a minute and take out) and keep aside. This will reduce the bitterness of the fenugreek leaves but keep their nutritional benefits intact.

Coriander (*Dhania*) powder- 1 teaspoon

Kashmiri Red Chilli powder–1/2 tea spoon (Recommended for colour, but if you like your dish to be really spicy, use some other hotter red chilli powder)

Fenugreek (*methi*) seeds- 1 teaspoon

Onion- 1 (chopped)

Garlic- 6 cloves (chopped)

Tomatoes- 2 (chopped)

Salt-1 tea spoon (or to taste)

Cooking Oil- 2 table spoon

Method

In a wok, pour the cooking oil, and place it on your heat source.

As the oil heats up, add the fenugreek seeds.

As soon as the fenugreek seeds turn brown, which takes just a few seconds (do please make sure they don't burn), add the chopped onion and garlic.

Stir till the onions become translucent. Now add the potatoes and stir till they start turning a golden brown in colour. Now add the red chilli, coriander powder and the salt. Stir well.

Now add the blanched fenugreek leaves and let these all cook together for about a minute.

Now add the tomatoes and cook till they are done.

That's all. Your Potato with fenugreek leaves dish is ready.

Prep time: 30 minutes (including for boiling the potatoes and for picking and blanching the fenugreek leaves)

Cooking time: 10 minutes

Total time: 40 minutes

Baigun Bhaja (Aubergine Fries)

This is a great Bengali (Eastern Indian) preparation that goes really well with the Eastern Indian *Khichdi*.

Serves 3-4

Ingredients

Fat round purple Aubergine-1

Turmeric (*Haldi*) powder-1 teaspoon

Salt- 1 teaspoon or to taste

Rice flour-1 tablespoon full

Mustard Oil -3 tablespoon

Method

Finely slice the aubergine into round pieces.

Sprinkle the salt and turmeric on both sides.

Sprinkle the rice flour and again let it cover all pieces on all sides well.

In a non-stick frying pan, heat the oil and add the aubergine pieces.

Let it brown on one side and then turn it over and brown the other side equally well.

(If you need to handle more aubergines, then fry them batch wise.)

Gently remove from the pan and put it in a dish lined with an absorbent paper napkin. This helps in soaking up the excess oil from the aubergine.

Put these in a serving dish and enjoy your *baigun bhaja.*

Prep time: 5 minutes

Cooking time: 2 minutes@ each batch of aubergines to be fried

Total time: Approximately 12-15 minutes

Bihari Style *Baingan Bharta* (Mashed Aubergines)

This typically Eastern Indian, or rather Bihari, dish is another dish that has to be served with *Littis* (Bihari baked bread) or *Khichdi*.

Serves 3-4

Ingredients

Aubergines (whole) – 2 approx. 1/2 kg (18oz) (2 cups)

Onion-1 (chopped finely)

Green chilli de-seeded (for flavour)-1 (Retain the seeds if you like it hot)

Fresh Coriander (*Dhania*) leaves-50 grams (2oz) (3 tablespoon)

Mustard oil (if you want the authentic flavour)-1/2 teaspoon

Salt-1/2 teaspoon or to taste

Method

Gently roast the aubergines directly on your heat source (i.e. without using any pans or utensils) till they are roasted well on all sides.

When the aubergines are cool to touch, peel away their somewhat burnt skin and discard.

Now put the cooked aubergines in a bowl and mash well with a fork.

Add the salt, mustard oil, onion, chillies and coriander (all raw).

Mix well.

That's all. Your Bihari *Baigan Bharta* is ready.

Prep time: 5 minutes

Cooking time: 15 minutes

Total time: 20 minutes

Punjabi Style *Baingan Bharta* (Mashed Aubergines)

This popular Punjabi dish can be had at most Indian restaurants and goes really with *rotis* or *parathas.*

Serves 3-4

Ingredients

Aubergines (whole) – 2 approx. 1/2 kg (18oz) (2 cups)

Onion-1 (chopped)

Garlic- 6 cloves (chopped)

Ginger- 1 inch (chopped)

Tomatoes- 2 (chopped)

Coriander (*Dhania*) powder- 1 teaspoon

Turmeric (*Haldi*) powder- ½ teaspoon

Kashmiri Red Chilli powder–1/2 tea spoon (Recommended for colour, but if you like your dish to be really spicy, use some other hotter red chilli powder)

Garam Masala-1/2 teaspoon

Tip: If you can't get ready-made *garam masala* mixture from a nearby Indian store, you can make yours by using 1 black cardamom, 3 green

cardamoms, 4 cloves, and 1 inch cinnamon-all ground together for this dish.

Green chilli de-seeded (for flavour)-1 (Retain the seeds if you like it hot)

Fresh Coriander (*Dhania*) leaves-50 grams (2oz) (3 tablespoon)

Mustard oil (if you want the authentic flavour) or any cooking oil-1 tablespoon

Salt-1/2 teaspoon or to taste

Method

Gently roast the aubergines directly on your heat source (i.e. without using any pans or utensils) till they are roasted well on all sides.

When the aubergines are cool to touch, peel away their somewhat burnt skin and discard.

Now put the cooked aubergines in a bowl and mash well with a fork.

Place a wok/deep pan on your heat source and pour in the cooking oil.

As soon as the oil heats up, add the onions, garlic and ginger.

Sauté till they start giving out a nice aroma.

Now add the tomatoes, salt, turmeric, coriander powder, red chilli powder and *garam masala*.

Stir well.

As soon as the tomatoes start cooking, add the mashed aubergines.

Mix well.

Switch off the heat source.

Garnish with fresh coriander leaves and green chilli.

That's all. Your Punjabi *Baigan Bharta* is ready.

Prep time: 5 minutes

Cooking time: 20 minutes

Total time: 25 minutes

Gatta (Chick Pea Flour Patties)

This is a classic Western Indian dish, from the deserts of Rajasthan, where in the absence of fresh greens you are forced to make do with just chick pea flour. But you have to doff your hat to the Rajasthanis for coming up with such a delicious dish even in such difficult circumstances.

Serves 3-4

Ingredients

Split Chick-pea flour (*Besan*)-2 cup (500 grams)

Turmeric (*Haldi*) powder –1/2 tea spoon

Dry crushed coriander (*Dhania*)-1 tea spoon

Kashmiri Red Chilli powder—1/2 tea spoon (Recommended for colour, but if you like your dish to be really spicy, use any other red chilli powder)

Asafoetida (*Hing*) - ½ teaspoon

Salt- 1 tea spoon (or to taste)

Cooking oil- enough to deep fry

Water-1/2 cup

Method

Mix together all the ingredients, along with the water, EXCEPT for the cooking oil, and knead well.

Set aside for 15 minutes.

Take the mixture in your hands and make 6" long sausage shaped patties.

In a muslin cloth, place all these patties, and tie a knot.

In a pan put two cups of water and bring it to a boil.

Place the muslin cloth with the patties in the boiling water and cook for 5 minutes.

Remove the patties from the water and let them cool down.

With a knife, cut the patties in to 1" round pieces and keep aside.

Heat oil in a wok/deep sauce pan and deep fry the round pieces till they turn a nice golden brown.

Take out on a plate lined with a paper napkin to absorb the excess oil.

That's all. Your Dry *Gattas* are ready.

Prep time: 20 minutes (including time for the mixture to set)

Cooking time: 10 minutes

Total time: 30 minutes

Dhokha (Chick Pea Flour Patties)

This is a Bihari (Eastern Indian) variation of the Rajasthani *Gattas*. Because in taste it mimics the popular fish fry, the locals call it *Dhokha* or deception!

Serves 3-4

Ingredients

Split Chick-pea flour (*Besan*)-2 cup (500 grams)

Turmeric (*Haldi*) powder –1/2 tea spoon

Dry crushed coriander (*Dhania*)-1 tea spoon

Kashmiri Red Chilli powder—1/2 tea spoon (Recommended for colour, but if you like your dish to be really spicy, use any other red chilli powder)

Asafoetida (*Hing*) - ½ teaspoon

Garlic- 8 cloves (crushed)

Mustard Paste- 2 tablespoon

Salt- 1 tea spoon (or to taste)

Cooking oil- enough to deep fry

Water-1 cup

Method

Mix together all the ingredients, along with the water, EXCEPT for the cooking oil.

Set aside for 15 minutes.

Place a wok/deep sauce pan on your heat source and add 1 tablespoon of cooking oil.

As soon as the oil heats up, add the *besan* mixture and keep stirring till the mixture becomes dry.

Remove to a plate and flatten it. Allow this to cool down.

Cut rectangular pieces.

Heat oil in a wok/deep sauce pan and deep fry these rectangular pieces till they turn a nice golden brown.

Take out on a plate lined with a paper napkin to absorb the excess oil.

That's all. Your *Dhokhas* are ready.

Prep time: 20 minutes (including time for the mixture to set)

Cooking time: 10 minutes

Total time: 30 minutes

Gaajar-Mattar Sabzi (Carrot and Peas Veggies)

Another simple North Indian dish that you can even have with your breakfast alongside your toast and egg.

Serves 3-4

Ingredients

Green peas (shelled, fresh are preferred) –200 grams (7oz) (1 cup)

Carrot–3 (cut into bite size pieces)

Kashmiri Red Chilli powder–1/4 tea spoon (Recommended for colour, but if you like your dish to be really spicy, use some other red chilli powder)

Cumin (*Jeera*) whole-1/2 tea spoon

Salt-1 level tea spoon (or to taste)

Ghee (clarified butter)-2 tea spoon

Method

Heat the *ghee* in a wok/ pan.

Add cumin to the *ghee* and as it turns brown, add the carrot and the peas.

Stir well.

Add all the chilli powder and salt to this mixture and reduce the heat.

Cover the wok/pan with a lid and let the vegetables cook for about 5 minutes.

Occasionally open the lid and stir so that the vegetables are not burnt.

The moment the vegetables are cooked to your liking, turn off the heat source.

Prep time: 5 minutes

Cooking time: 7 minutes

Total time: 12 minutes

Chapter 3: Veggie Curries

"In our gardens, Lord Ganesha sends His power through fruits and vegetables, the ones that grow above the ground, to permeate our nerve system with wisdom, clearing obstacles in our path when eaten. The growers of them treat it like they would care for Ganesha in His physical form."

–Ancient Hindu Belief

Indian cuisine is famous for its curries, so much so that in Britain many Indian restaurants are simply called "Curry Houses".

Condescending though it may sound, Indians shouldn't really complain because anywhere you go, you will find curries dominating the Indian meal platter.

Why is it so?

One reason could be the need to have lots of water in a tropical country like India. This curries could meet in a very healthy (you are boiling your water after all, aren't you) and appetising a manner.

The second reason could be that if you are growing so much rice, you would need some curry to "wet" it, to make it less sticky and more palatable.

This could be a reason that you have curries in all rice-growing regions of the world, even in Thailand, Laos or Myanmar. On the other hand, the non-rice growing and wheat-eating colder areas of China, Afghanistan and Central Asia rely more on barbeques and naans. So they don't seem to have much need for curries.

Curries are NOT Sauces: It is common practice in Western cuisine to boil or bake something first and then to pour on it a tomato or cheese based sauce. Or flambé it with some wine or such other alcoholic beverage.

Yes, Indian restaurants do semi cook their meats and vegetables and prepare some sauces separately. Both are to be mixed the moment someone asks for a tomato or onion or yoghurt based dish. This is for practical considerations because for restaurants, speed is of utmost essence. So they have to keep ingredients ready in a semi-finished condition for a quick conversion in to whatever dishes the customers demand.

However, "Home Style" (or even *dhaba* or wayside eatery) Indian food is made in one go with everything cooked together. The only thing to "finish" a curry dish could then be the sprinkling of some fresh Coriander (Cilantro) leaves.

With this little introduction, let me present to you 26 outstanding "Home Style" vegetable curries from almost every corner of India.

There are in all 13 North-Indian, 9 East Indian, 2 Western, and 2 South Indian dishes. Master these and you can rustle up any other vegetable dish from any part of India.

Band Gobi, Gaajar, Aloo, Mattar ki Sabzi (Cabbage, Carrot, Potatoes and Peas Curry)

This is a great medley of popular winter vegetables of India. You can, of course, follow this recipe to make your own medley of favourite veggies.

Serves 3-4

Ingredients

Cabbage–1/2 Kg (500 grams or 18oz or 2 cups)

Green peas (shelled, fresh are preferred)–200 grams (7oz) (1 cup)

Potatoes-2 (chopped)

Carrots–2 (chopped)

Medium size Onions–2 (chopped)

Garlic-4 cloves

Ginger-1 inch

Fresh tomatos-2 (chopped)

Turmeric (*Haldi*) powder- 1/2 tea spoon

Dry crushed coriander (*Dhania*) powder-2 tea spoons

Garam Masala (mixture of common Indian spices) crushed- 1/2 tea spoon

Tip: If you can't get ready-made *garam masala* mixture from a nearby Indian store, you can make yours by using 1 black cardamom, 3 green cardamoms, 4 cloves, and 1 inch cinnamon-all ground together.

Kashmiri Red Chilli powder–1/4 tea spoon (Recommended for colour, but if you like your dish to be really spicy, use some other hotter red chilli powder)

Cumin (*Jeera*) whole-1/2 tea spoon

Salt-1 level tea spoon (or to taste)

Tomato Ketchup-1 table spoon

Cooking oil-1 table spoon

Ghee (clarified butter)-1 tea spoon

Water-1 cup (200 ml)

Method using a pressure cooker

Blend together (in a blender preferably!) the onions, garlic, ginger and tomatoes to a fine paste.

Cut cabbage, carrots and potatoes somewhat roughly so that they retain their crunchiness even after they are cooked.

Now pour the oil in a pressure cooker and put it on your heat source.

As the oil heats up, add cumin seeds.

As these splutter and turn brown, add the paste from the blender and gently fry it.

As the paste starts giving off a nice aroma, add all the vegetables (cabbage, carrot, peas and potatoes) and sauté gently.

Add all the dry condiments and salt to this mixture and keep stirring till all the vegetables are well coated.

Add now the ketchup and *ghee* to the mixture and stir again.

Add the water.

Close the lid with weight and bring it to full pressure on high heat, that is, when the weight lifts and there is a whistling sound.

Immediately turn off the heat source.

Let the cooker cool down on its own before opening it.

That's all. Your *band gobi, gaajar, aloo matter sabzi* (cabbage, carrot, potatoes and peas curry) is ready.

Method using a wok/deep sauce pan

Blend together (in a blender preferably!) the onions, garlic, ginger and tomatoes to a fine paste.

Cut cabbage, carrots and potatoes somewhat roughly so that they retain their crunchiness even after they are cooked.

Now pour the oil in a wok/deep sauce pan and put it on your heat source.

As the oil heats up, add cumin seeds.

As these splutter and turn brown, add the paste from the blender and gently fry it.

As the paste starts giving off a nice aroma, add all the vegetables (cabbage, carrot, peas and potatoes) and sauté gently.

Add all the dry condiments and salt to this mixture and keep stirring till all the vegetables are well coated.

Add now the ketchup and *ghee* to the mixture and stir again.

Add the water.

Now cover the wok/deep pan with a lid and reduce the heat to minimum. Let the vegetables cook to your liking for about 10 minutes. You may poke the vegetables once in a while with a fork to see whether they have been fully cooked.

You can now turn off the heat source.

That's all. Your *band gobi, gaajar, aloo matter sabzi* (cabbage, carrot, potatoes and peas curry) is ready.

Prep time: 10 minutes

Cooking time: 7 minutes with pressure cooker; 15-20 minutes with a wok/deep pan

Total time: 17 minutes with pressure cooker; 25-30 minutes with a wok/deep pan

Mattar Paneer (Indian Cottage Cheese with Peas in a Curry)

This is the classic North Indian dish that you will find everywhere, in homes, *dhabas* as well as fancy restaurants. Here is a low calorie version, however.

Serves 3-4

Ingredients

Paneer (Cottage cheese)–1/2 Kg (500 grams or 18oz or 2 cups)

Green peas (shelled, fresh are preferred)–200 grams (7oz) (1 cup)

Medium size Onions--2

Garlic-4 cloves

Ginger-1 inch

Fresh tomato-2 (washed and chopped)

Turmeric (*Haldi*) - 1/2 tea spoon

Dry crushed Coriander (*Dhania*)-2 tea spoons

Garam Masala (mixture of common Indian spices) crushed- 1/2 tea spoon

Tip: If you can't get ready-made *garam masala* mixture from a nearby Indian store, you can make yours by using 1 black cardamom, 3 green

cardamoms, 4 cloves, and 1 inch cinnamon-all ground together.

Kashmiri Red Chilli powder–1/4 tea spoon (Recommended for colour, but if you like your dish to be really spicy, use some other hotter red chilli powder)

Cumin (*Jeera*) whole-1/2 tea spoon

Salt-1 level tea spoon (or to taste)

Tomato Ketchup-1 table spoon

Cooking oil-1 table spoon

Ghee (clarified butter)-1 tea spoon

Water-1 cup (200 ml)

Method using a pressure cooker

Take the full block of *paneer* (cottage cheese) and dry roast it on a non-stick pan till it turns a golden brown. Then cut it into bite size pieces.

(Most recipes would advise that you fry these pieces in oil, which you can try if you don't mind the additional calories!)

Blend together (in a blender preferably!) the onions, garlic, ginger and tomatoes to a fine paste.

Now pour the oil in a pressure cooker and put it on your heat source.

Add cumin to the oil and as it turns brown, add this paste and gently fry the same.

As the paste starts giving off a nice aroma, add the peas and the cottage cheese and sauté gently.

Add all the dry condiments (masala) and salt to this mixture.

Add the ketchup and *ghee* to the mixture and stir again.

Add the water, close the lid with weight and bring it to full pressure on high heat, that is, when the weight lifts and there is a whistling sound.

Switch off the heat source and release the pressure immediately, otherwise the veggies will be overcooked.

Let the cooker cool down on its own before opening it.

That's all. Your *Mattar Paneer* (cottage cheese with peas curry) is ready.

Method using a wok/deep sauce pan

Take the full block of *paneer* (cottage cheese) and dry roast it on a non- stick pan till it turns a golden brown. Then cut it into bite size pieces.

(Most recipes would advise that you fry these pieces in oil, which you can try if you don't mind the additional calories!)

Blend together (in a blender preferably!) the onions, garlic, ginger and tomatoes to a fine paste.

Now pour the oil in a wok/deep sauce pan and put it on your heat source.

Add cumin to the oil and as it turns brown, add this paste and gently fry the same.

As the paste starts giving off a nice aroma, add the peas and the cottage cheese and sauté gently.

Add all the dry condiments (masala) and salt to this mixture.

Add the ketchup and *ghee* to the mixture and stir again.

Add the water, cover the wok/pan with a lid and reduce the heat to minimum. Let the peas cook to your liking, which should take about 5 minutes.

Switch off the heat source.

That's all. Your *Mattar Paneer* (cottage cheese with peas curry) is ready.

Prep time: 10 minutes

Cooking time: 5 minutes with pressure cooker, 10 minutes with a wok/pan

Total time: 15 minutes with pressure cooker, 20 minutes with a wok/pan

Mixed Vegetables in Coconut Milk

If you want to be really adventurous, try making this South Indian mixed vegetable curry in coconut milk. Believe me, it tastes so heavenly that it will soon become your personal favourite.

In addition, this 6-vegetable recipe with the goodness of coconut milk and so many Indian spices is oozing with health benefits from all its pores.

Serves 3-4

Ingredients

Yellow Pumpkin-150 grams (5oz) (half cup)

Carrot-100 grams (3.5oz) (half cup)

Beans-100 grams (3.5oz) (half cup)

Cauliflower-100 grams (3.5oz) (half cup)

Potato-100 grams (3.5oz) (half cup)

Bottle Gourd-100 grams (3.5oz) (half cup)

Onion-1

Ginger-1 inch

Garlic-4 cloves

Tomato-1

(Onion+ Ginger+ Garlic + tomato to be made into a fine paste in a blender)

Black Mustard (*Rai*) seeds-1/2 teaspoon

Curry leaves-a few

Coriander (*Dhania*) powder-2 teaspoon

Turmeric (*Haldi*) powder-1 teaspoon

Kashmiri Red Chilli powder–1/4 tea spoon (Recommended for colour, but if you like your dish to be really spicy, use some other hotter red chilli powder)

Coconut milk-400 ml (1 + ½ cups)

Cooking oil-2 tablespoon

Salt- 1 level tea spoon (or to taste)

Method using a pressure cooker

Wash and cut the vegetables into bite size pieces.

Prepare your onion + garlic+ ginger + tomato paste.

 Now place the pressure cooker on your heat source and add the cooking oil.

When the oil warms up, add the mustard seeds (*rai*) and the curry leaves.

When the *rai* splutters, add the onion + garlic+ ginger + tomato paste. Stir well.

Keep stirring till the paste is well fried and gives off a lovely aroma.

Note: Instead of making and frying the onion, garlic, ginger and tomato paste, you can certainly use some ready-made fried paste, if you can manage to get that. This would save a lot of time as you don't have to first blend and then brown the onion + garlic+ ginger + tomato paste.

Add all the vegetables to this mixture and stir well.

Add the coriander, turmeric, red chilli powder and the salt.

Keep stirring till all the vegetables are well coated.

Now, add a little water and close the lid of the cooker.

Put the weight and let the cooker come to full pressure, that is, when the weight lifts and there is a whistling sound.

Switch off the heat source and release the pressure immediately, otherwise the veggies will be overcooked.

Open the lid and now add the coconut milk.

Switch on the heat source and put the cooker back on it once again (without covering it) till the vegetables come to a boil.

You can now finally switch off the heat source.

That's all. Your mixed vegetables in coconut milk is ready to be served.

Method using a wok/deep sauce pan

Wash and cut the vegetables into bite size pieces.

Prepare your onion + garlic+ ginger + tomato paste.

Now place the wok/pan on your heat source and add the cooking oil.

When the oil warms up, add the mustard seeds (*rai*) and the curry leaves.

When the *rai* splutters, add the onion + garlic+ ginger + tomato paste. Stir well.

Keep stirring till the paste is well fried and gives off a lovely aroma.

Note: Instead of making and frying the onion, garlic, ginger and tomato paste, you can certainly use some ready-made fried paste, if you can manage to get that. This would save a lot of time as you don't have to first blend and then brown the onion + garlic+ ginger + tomato paste.

Add all the vegetables to this mixture and stir well.

Add the coriander, turmeric, red chilli powder and the salt.

Keep stirring till all the vegetables are well coated.

Now, add a little water, cover the wok/deep pan with a lid and reduce the heat to minimum.

Let the vegetables cook to your liking for about 10 minutes.

You may poke the vegetables once in a while with a fork to see that they have been cooked well.

Open the cover and now add the coconut milk.

Stir lightly and let the vegetables come to a boil.

You can now switch off the heat source.

That's all. Your mixed vegetables in coconut milk is ready to be served.

Prep time: 10 minutes

Cooking time: 7 minutes with a pressure cooker, 15 minutes with wok/pan

Total time: 17 minutes with a pressure cooker, 25 minutes with wok/pan

Palak Paneer (Indian Cottage Cheese in Pureed Spinach Curry)

Another very popular North Indian (Punjabi) dish that can be made as mild (or spicy) as you like it. This recipe is ideal for introducing the benefits of the humble spinach to the young members of your family, and that too in a really delicious manner.

Serves 3-4

Ingredients

Paneer (Cottage cheese)–1/2 Kg (500 grams or 18oz or 2 cups)

Spinach–1 Kg (2lb) (4 cups) washed well

Medium size Onions—1 (chopped)

Garlic-4 cloves

Fresh tomato-1 (chopped)

Garam Masala (mixture of common Indian spices) crushed- 1/2 tea spoon

Tip: If you can't get ready-made *garam masala* mixture from a nearby Indian store, you can make yours by using 1 black cardamom, 3 green cardamoms, 4 cloves, and 1 inch cinnamon-all ground together.

Kashmiri Red Chilli powder–1/4 tea spoon (Recommended for colour, but if you like your dish to

be really spicy, use some other hotter red chilli powder)

Cumin seeds (*Jeera*)-1/2 tea spoon

Salt- 1 level tea spoon (or to taste)

Ghee (clarified butter)-2 tablespoon

Method using a pressure cooker

Take the full block of *paneer* (cottage cheese) and dry roast it on a non-stick pan till it turns a golden brown. Then cut it into bite size pieces.

(Most recipes would advise that you fry these pieces in oil, which you can try if you don't mind the additional calories!)

In a pressure cooker, put together the washed spinach, onions, garlic and tomatoes and put it on your heat source.

Please note that there is no need to add any water as spinach leaves a lot of water.

Now bring the cooker to full pressure, that is, when the weight lifts and there is a whistling sound.

Remove the pressure cooker from your heat source, cool it under running cold water and release the pressure.

Pour all the cooked ingredients from the pressure cooker into a blender and blend well.

Place a clean wok on your heat source.

Add the clarified butter (*Ghee*).

As the clarified butter warms up, add the cumin seeds (*Jeera*).

When the *Jeera* starts to brown, add the blended spinach mixture.

Thereafter add the *garam masala*, the red chilli powder and the salt. Mix well.

Add the roasted cottage cheese now and let the curry come to a boil.

Switch off the heat source.

That's all. Your *Palak Paneer* is ready.

Relish this with rice or *rotis*.

Method using a wok/deep sauce pan

Take the full block of *paneer* (cottage cheese) and dry roast it on a non-stick pan till it turns a golden brown. Then cut it into bite size pieces.

(Most recipes would advise that you fry these pieces in oil, which you can try if you don't mind the additional calories!)

In a wok/pan, put together the washed spinach, onions, garlic and tomatoes and put it on your heat source.

Put ½ a cup of water and cover with a lid. Please note that there is no need to add any more water as spinach leaves a lot of water.

The moment you see the juices boiling, reduce the heat to minimum and let the spinach cook for approximately 10 minutes in its own juice.

Pour all the cooked ingredients from the wok/deep pan into a blender and blend well.

Place a clean wok (and not the one used for boiling the ingredients, unless you clean that first) on your heat source.

Add the clarified butter (*ghee*).

As the clarified butter warms up, add the cumin seeds (*jeera*).

When the *jeera* starts to brown, add the blended spinach mixture.

Thereafter add the *garam masala*, the red chilli powder and the salt. Mix well.

Add the roasted cottage cheese now and let the curry come to a boil. Switch off the heat source.

That's all. Your *Palak Paneer* is ready.

Relish this with rice or *rotis*.

Prep time: 5 minutes

Cooking time: 20 minutes with pressure cooker, 30 minutes with wok/deep pan

Total time: 25 minutes with pressure cooker, 35 minutes with wok/deep pan

---

Sarson Ka Saag (Mustard Leaves Dish)

This is another classic North Indian (Punjabi) dish that goes well with *Makki di Roti* (Corn flour bread) or *Missi Roti* (Chick pea flour bread). Try this recipe when you want to put some zing to the humble spinach.

Serves 3-4

Ingredients

Mustard leaves (*Sarson ka saag*)-1 Kg (2lb) (4 cups)

Spinach-300 grams or 10oz (1 cup) (This is added to reduce the somewhat bitter taste of the mustard leaves.)

Chopped Onions-2

Garlic-4 cloves

Chopped Tomatoes-3

Turmeric (*Haldi*)-1/2 teaspoon

Kashmiri Red Chilli powder–1/2 tea spoon (Recommended for colour, but if you like your dish to be really spicy, use some other hotter red chilli powder)

Cumin seeds (*jeera*)-1/2 teaspoon

Mustard Oil (preferred for the authentic taste, otherwise feel free to use your preferred cooking oil)-1 tablespoon

Clarified Butter (*ghee*)-1 tablespoon

Salt- 1 level tea spoon (or to taste)

Water-1/2 cup

Method using a pressure cooker

Wash and chop the mustard leaves, spinach, 1 onion (of two), all the four garlic cloves and 2 tomatoes (out of 3).

Place these in a pressure cooker with ½ cup water.

Switch on the heat source and bring the pressure cooker to full pressure, that is, when the weight lifts and there is a whistling sound.

 Switch off the heat.

When the ingredients in the cooker cool down, put them in a blender and blend well.

Place a clean wok on your heat source.

Add the oil and clarified butter (*ghee*).

When this warms up, add the cumin seeds (*jeera*).

As soon as the seeds brown, add the left over chopped onions and fry well till the onions acquire a nice golden colour.

Now add the left over tomato, the chilli powder and turmeric (*haldi*).

Sauté well till the tomatoes soften up.

Add the blended ingredients and the salt.

Let the mixture come to a boil.

Switch off the heat source.

That's all. Your Mustard Spinach leaves dish (*Sarson Ka Saag*) is ready.

It tastes really good with most Indian breads, especially *Missi* (chick pea flour) *roti*.

Method using a wok/deep sauce pan

Wash and chop the mustard leaves, spinach, 1 onion (of two), all the four garlic cloves and 2 tomatoes (out of 3).

Place these in a wok/pan with ½ cup water.

Switch on the heat source and the moment the water starts boiling, reduce the heat to the minimum and let the spinach-mustard leaves combo cook for approximately 5 more minutes in its own juice.

Switch off the heat.

When the ingredients in the wok/pan cool down, put them in a blender and blend well.

Place a clean wok (and not the one used for boiling the ingredients, unless you clean that first) on your heat source.

Add the oil and clarified butter (*ghee*).

When this warms up, add the cumin seeds (*jeera*).

As soon as the seeds brown, add the left over chopped onions and fry well till the onions acquire a nice golden colour.

Now add the left over tomato, the chilli powder and turmeric (*haldi*).

Sauté well till the tomatoes soften up.

Add the blended ingredients and the salt.

Let the mixture come to a boil.

Switch off the heat source.

That's all. Your Mustard Spinach leaves dish (*Sarson Ka Saag*) is ready.

It tastes really good with most Indian breads, especially *Missi* (chick pea flour) *roti*.

Prep time: 10 minutes

Cooking time: 15 minutes with pressure cooker; 20 minutes with a wok/deep pan

Total time: 25 minutes with pressure cooker; 35 minutes with a wok/deep pan

Rajma Aloo (Red Kidney Beans Potato Curry)

A perennial favourite of the North Indian states of Punjab, Haryana, Himachal Pradesh and Jammu & Kashmir, this dish is cooked more like meat than lentils. Many wayside eateries or *dhabas* thrive on serving just *Rajma* with fragrant Basmati rice and readily find a seemingly never ending queue of diners.

Try this dish once and you will not touch that can of insipid Baked Beans with tomato sauce ever again.

Serves 3-4

Ingredients

Red Kidney beans (*Rajma*)-1 small cup

Water-4 cups (same cup as above!)

Potato- 3 (peeled and cut into 4 pieces each)

Chopped Onion-1

Chopped Garlic-5 cloves

Chopped Ginger-1 inch (2.5 cm or 1/3rd length of a finger) piece

Chopped Tomatoes-4

Garam Masala powder-1/2 teaspoon

Tip: If you can't get ready-made *garam masala* mixture from a nearby Indian store, you can make yours by using 1 black cardamom, 3 green cardamoms, 4 cloves, and 1 inch cinnamon-all ground together.

Turmeric (*haldi*)-1/2 teaspoon

Cumin seeds (*jeera*)-1/2 teaspoon

Kashmiri Red Chilli powder–1/2 tea spoon (Recommended for colour, but if you like your dish to be really spicy, use some other hotter red chilli powder)

Clarified butter (*ghee*)-2 tablespoon

Salt- 1 level teaspoon or to taste

Sugar-1/4 teaspoon

Method

Soak the kidney beans overnight in 2 cups of water.

Note: If you don't pre-soak the beans, the cooking time will be extremely long and the beans may not cook that easily.

Place the pressure cooker on your heat source.

Add the clarified butter and when it melts, add the cumin seeds.

As soon as the cumin seeds turn brown, which takes just a few seconds (do please make sure they don't burn), add the chopped onion, garlic and ginger.

Sauté well till the onions become translucent and start giving a nice aroma.

Add the kidney beans, and the potatoes along with the chilli powder, turmeric powder, *garam masala*, salt and sugar.

Sauté for about a minute.

To this mixture, now add the tomatoes.

Roast well till the tomatoes are cooked.

Now add 4 cups of water and close the lid.

Let the cooker come to full pressure i.e. when steam starts escaping from the vent (don't worry, you will hear that typical sound), and then immediately reduce the heat to minimum.

In other words, if cooking on gas, turn the knob to SIM (mer).

Cook on low heat for 15 minutes more.

Thereafter turn off the heat source and let the cooker cool on its own.

Open the lid and see if the rajma has the desired consistency.

In case you want it to be more wettish, you can add some more water.

In case you want it drier, then you can put it back on the heat source without the lid and let the water evaporate.

While doing either, please remember to keep stirring, so that the rajma does not burn.

This dish goes really well with plain, long grain Basmati rice.

Prep time: 5 minutes (excluding overnight soaking time)

Cooking time: 20 minutes with pressure cooker

Total time: 25 minutes

Chhola (Whole Chick Pea Curry)

This is another classic dish of the North Indian states of Punjab, Haryana, Himachal Pradesh and Jammu & Kashmir. Again, like *Rajma*, this dish too is cooked more like meat than lentils. However, unlike *Rajma* which is traditionally enjoyed with fragrant Basmati rice, *chhola* is paired more with *pooris* (fried and puffed up Indian unleavened bread) and *bhathuras* (another variation of fried and puffed up Indian leavened bread). This combo is in fact quite a favourite for breakfasts or rather brunches.

Try this dish with rice or any kind of bread, Western or Indian, and I bet you will fall in love with it.

Serves 3-4

Ingredients

Whole white chick pea (*Kabuli Chana* or *Chhola*)-1 small cup

Onions-2

Garlic-6 cloves

Ginger-1+1/2 inches (4 cm or 2/3rd length of a finger) piece

Tomatoes-3

Cumin seeds (*Jeera*)-1/2 teaspoon

Coriander (*Dhania*) powder-2 teaspoon

Turmeric (*Haldi*) powder- 1 teaspoon

Garam Masala powder-1/2 teaspoon

Tip: If you can't get ready-made *garam masala* mixture from a nearby Indian store, you can make yours by using 1 black cardamom, 3 green cardamoms, 4 cloves, and 1 inch cinnamon-all ground together.

Kashmiri Red Chilli powder–1/2 tea spoon (Recommended for colour, but if you like your dish to be really spicy, use some other hotter red chilli powder)

Cooking Oil- 2 tablespoon

Salt- 1 level teaspoon or to taste

Method

Soak the chick pea in a vessel with water (which covers the chick peas completely) at least for 4 hours. This way when you cook the chick peas, they become nice and tender and take less time to cook.

Put the pre-soaked chick peas in a pressure cooker, with enough water to cover the chick peas.

Switch on the heat source and close the lid of the pressure cooker with weight.

When the cooker comes to full pressure, i.e. when steam starts escaping from the vent (don't worry, you will hear that typical sound), reduce the heat (to Sim on a gas stove) and let the chick peas cook for 10 minutes more.

Turn off the heat source and let the cooker cool down.

In a grinder, make a fine paste of the tomatoes, ginger, garlic and onion.

Place a wok on a heat source and add the cooking oil.

When the oil warms up, add the cumin seeds.

In a few seconds, as soon as the cumin seeds turn brown, add the paste you have just made in the grinder. Do please ensure that the cumin seeds do not burn.

Sauté the paste till it starts giving a nice aroma.

Now add the turmeric powder, *garam masala*, red chilli powder and coriander powder.

Sauté for another 2 minutes.

Now, add the chick peas (without the water) to this mixture.

Mix well and add the salt.

You can now add as much water as you like depending upon the thickness of the curry that you want.

Let the mixture boil for about 2 minutes so that all the ingredients are well blended.

That's all. Your *Chhola* is ready.

Prep time: 5 minutes (excluding soaking time)

Cooking time: 20 minutes with pressure cooker

Total time: 25 minutes

Note: If you have sampled *chhola* in a *dhaba*, you may find my "Home Style" recipe a little mild. This is for two main reasons.

First, since the *dhabas* have to cook huge quantities (say 10 Kgs or 22 lbs of chick Peas in one go), and that too in big non-pressurised vessels, they slip in some baking soda to their pre-soaking process.

I'm NOT in favour of this practice because this unnecessarily increases the sodium levels of your *chhola* (which is bad for your blood pressure) without enhancing the taste.

In fact, the somewhat soapy taste that baking soda imparts to this dish may not suit sensitive palates.

Which leads to the second point, of drowning this baking soda induced flavour. This is done by using stronger spices like *Kastoori Methi* (fragrant Fenugreek).

Then *Anardana* (ground seeds of wild pomegranate) is used to increase the tanginess of the dish.

Finally, used tea leaves are added to impart a blackish colour to the *chhola*, which some traditionalists like!

I have nothing against the second or the third points. Use these if you crave the authentic *dhaba* flavour.

But for the first, you may be better off using a pressure cooker or a slow cooker than using baking soda.

Incidentally, if you wish to do away with the use of a wok in this recipe, you can use the exact methodology as given for the previous recipe for *rajma* (with or without potatoes).

Sambar

The South Indian states of Andhra Pradesh, Tamil Nadu, Karnataka and Kerala prefer to cook their *Arhar/Toor dal* with this fiery but tasty twist. In fact, they love Sambar so much that they have to have it for all meals—breakfast, lunch and dinner!

Adding veggies to *Sambar* is a common practice that undoubtedly increases the nutritional quotient of this dish.

Be careful, this is NOT a mild lentil soup!

Serves 3-4

Ingredients

Arhar/Toor (split pigeon peas) Dal-1 small cup

Water-4 cups (same cup as above!)

Onion-1

Tomatoes-2

Garlic-6 cloves

Beans-100 grams (3.5oz) (half cup)

Pumpkin-100 grams (3.5oz) (half cup)

Bottle Gourd-100 grams (3.5oz) (half cup)

Sambar masala powder-4 teaspoon

Tip: If you can't get ready-made *Sambar masala* mixture from a nearby Indian store, you can make yours by one tablespoon coriander powder + 2 teaspoon cumin powder + ½ teaspoon ground black pepper + ½ teaspoon chilli powder + ½ teaspoon turmeric powder + ¼ teaspoon asafoetida—all mixed together.

Tamarind paste-1 tablespoon dissolved in 1/2 cup of water

Ghee-1 tablespoon

Black Mustard seeds (*Rai*)-1 teaspoon

Curry leaves-10-12

Salt- 1 level teaspoon or to taste

Sugar-1/2 teaspoon

Method

Wash the dal and vegetables well.

Chop up the vegetables, onion, tomatoes and garlic.

 In a pressure cooker, put the dal and the chopped vegetables along with the chopped onion, tomatoes and garlic.

Add the *sambar masala*, salt and sugar.

Add water.

Close the lid and put it on your heat source.

When the pressure cooker comes to full pressure (i.e. when the weight lifts and there is a whistling sound), reduce the heat (to SIM on a gas stove) and let it cook for 7 minutes more.

Let the cooker cool down on its own and then open it.

Add the tamarind paste and boil it once more without covering it with the lid.

In a tempering pan, add the *ghee*, the black mustard seeds and the curry leaves and put it on your heat source.

When the seeds splutter, add this mixture to the Sambar.

That's all. Your *Sambar* is ready.

Note: In case, you cannot get curry leaves, black mustard seeds alone can also impart the required flavour.

If you like your *Sambar* to taste more sour, you can add more tamarind paste. Similarly, if you want your Sambar to taste sweeter, you can add more sugar.

Prep time: 8 minutes for washing, chopping and collecting all ingredients

Cooking time: 12 minutes with pressure cooker

Total time: 20 minutes

Whole Green *Chana Ghugni* (Green Chick Pea Bihari Style Curry)

This is a very simple but tasty dish from the Eastern Indian state of Bihar.

Serves 3-4

Ingredients

Green *Chana* (chick pea) - ½ cup

Onion- 1 (chopped)

Tomato- 1 (chopped)

Cumin (*jeera*) seeds- ½ tea spoon

Cooking oil- 1 tea spoon

Water- 1 cup

Salt- ½ teaspoon or to taste

Method

Pre-soak the dried green chick pea in a vessel with water (which covers the green chick peas completely) at least for 4 hours. This way when you cook the chick peas, they become nice and tender and will take less time to cook.

(In case, you can lay your hands on farm fresh green chick pea, there would be neither any need to pre-soak nor pressure cook these.)

Place the pressure cooker on your heat source.

Add the cooking oil and when it warms up, add the cumin seeds.

As soon as the cumin seeds turn brown, which takes just a few seconds (do please make sure they don't burn), add the chopped onion, and the tomatoes.

Stir well till the onions become translucent and start giving a nice aroma.

Now add the green *chana*, salt and the water.

Close the lid of the pressure cooker with weight.

When the cooker comes to full pressure, i.e. when steam starts escaping from the vent (don't worry, you will hear that typical sound), reduce the heat (to Sim on a gas stove) and let the chick peas cook for 5 minutes more.

Turn off the heat source and let the cooker cool down.

That's all. Your Green *Chana Ghugni* is ready.

Prep time: 5 minutes (excluding soaking time)

Cooking time: 10 minutes with pressure cooker

Total time: 15 minutes

Green Peas and Potato *Ghugni* (Bihari Style Curry)

This is the favourite "Railway Station" dish all over North India that is usually served with *pooris* (fried and puffed up Indian bread).

Serves–2

Ingredients

Green Peas (shelled, fresh are preferred) - ½ cup (100 grams or 3.5 oz.)

Potato- 1 (cut into bite size pieces)

Tomato- 2 (chopped)

Cumin *(jeera)* seeds- ½ tea spoon

Cooking oil- 1 tea spoon

Water- 1/2 cup

Salt- ½ teaspoon or to taste

Method using a pressure cooker

Place the pressure cooker on your heat source.

Add the cooking oil and when it warms up, add the cumin seeds.

As soon as the cumin seeds turn brown, which takes just a few seconds (do please make sure they don't burn), add the peas, and the potato.

Stir well for about a minute and add the tomatoes.

Stir till the tomatoes are slightly cooked.

Now add salt and the water.

Close the lid of the pressure cooker with weight.

When the cooker comes to full pressure, i.e. when steam starts escaping from the vent (don't worry, you will hear that typical sound), turn off the heat source and let the cooker cool down.

That's all. Your Green Pea-Potato *Ghugni* is ready.

Method using a wok/deep sauce pan

Place the wok/deep sauce pan on your heat source.

Add the cooking oil and when it warms up, add the cumin seeds.

As soon as the cumin seeds turn brown, which takes just a few seconds (do please make sure they don't burn), add the peas, and the potato.

Stir well for about a minute and add the tomatoes.

Stir till the tomatoes are slightly cooked.

Add salt and the water.

Now cover the wok/deep pan with a lid and reduce the heat to minimum. Let the vegetables cook to your liking for about 10 minutes. You may poke the vegetables once in a while with a fork to see whether they have been fully cooked.

You can now turn off the heat source.

That's all. Your Green Pea-Potato *Ghugni* is ready.

Prep time: 5 minutes

Cooking time: 5 minutes with pressure cooker, 10 minutes with a wok/pan

Total time: 10 minutes with pressure cooker, 15 minutes with a wok/pan

Green Peas Dal (Bihari Style)

Yet another simple but tasty dish from the Eastern Indian state of Bihar.

Serves 3-4

Ingredients

Green Peas (shelled, fresh are preferred) - 1½ cup (300 grams or 10.5 oz.)

Tomato- 3 (chopped)

Cumin seeds (*Jeera*) - ½ tea spoon

Turmeric (*Haldi*) powder- ½ tea spoon

Kashmiri Red Chilli powder–1/4 tea spoon (Recommended for colour, but if you like your dish to be really spicy, use some other hotter red chilli powder)

Garam Masala-½ tea spoon

Tip: If you can't get ready-made *garam masala* mixture from a nearby Indian store, you can make yours by using 1 black cardamom, 3 green cardamoms, 4 cloves, and 1 inch cinnamon-all ground together.

Coriander (*Dhania*) powder-1 tea spoon

Ghee (clarified butter) - 1 table spoon

Water- 2 cups

Salt- 1 teaspoon or to taste

Method using a pressure cooker

In a blender, crush ½ cup green peas and keep aside.

Place the pressure cooker on your heat source.

Add the *ghee* and when it warms up, add the cumin seeds.

As soon as the cumin seeds turn brown, which takes just a few seconds (do please make sure they don't burn), add the peas, both crushed and whole.

Stir well for about a minute and add the tomatoes.

Stir till the tomatoes are slightly cooked.

Now add turmeric, coriander, red chilli powder, *garam masala* and salt.

Stir again for a minute. Add water.

Close the lid of the pressure cooker with weight.

When the cooker comes to full pressure, i.e. when steam starts escaping from the vent (don't worry, you will hear that typical sound), reduce the heat (to Sim on a gas stove) and let the peas cook for 5 minutes more.

Turn off the heat source and let the cooker cool down.

That's all. Your Green Peas Dal (Bihari style) is ready.

Method using a wok/deep sauce pan

In a blender, crush ½ cup green peas and keep aside.

Place the wok/pan on your heat source.

Add the *ghee* and when it warms up, add the cumin seeds.

As soon as the cumin seeds turn brown, which takes just a few seconds (do please make sure they don't burn), add the peas, both crushed and whole.

Stir well for about a minute and add the tomatoes.

Stir till the tomatoes are slightly cooked.

Now add turmeric, coriander, red chilli powder, *garam masala* and salt.

Stir again for a minute. Add water.

Now cover the wok/deep pan with a lid and reduce the heat to minimum. Let the peas cook to your liking for about 10 minutes. You may check once in a while with a fork to see whether they have been fully cooked.

Turn off the heat source.

That's all. Your Green Peas Dal (Bihari style) is ready.

Prep time: 7 minutes

Cooking time: 10 minutes with pressure cooker, 20 minutes with a wok/pan

Total time: 17 minutes with pressure cooker, 27 minutes with a wok/pan

Soya *Mattar* (Soya Granules-Peas Curry)

If you wish to infuse some "first class protein" in to your veggies, just try this simple dish.

Serves 3-4

Ingredients

Soya Granules—1 cup

Green peas (shelled fresh are preferred) –1/2 cup (100 grams or 3.5 oz.)

Medium size Onions–2 (chopped)

Garlic-4 cloves

Ginger-1 inch (2.5 cm or 1/3rd length of a finger)

Fresh tomato-2 (chopped)

Turmeric (*Haldi*) powder- 1/2 tea spoon

Dry crushed coriander (*Dhania*) powder–2 tea spoon

Garam Masala (mixture of common Indian spices) crushed- 1/2 tea spoon

Tip: If you can't get ready-made *garam masala* mixture from a nearby Indian store, you can make yours by using 1 black cardamom, 3 green cardamoms, 4 cloves, and 1 inch cinnamon—all ground together.

Kashmiri Red Chilli powder–1/4 tea spoon (Recommended for colour, but if you like your dish to be really spicy, use any other red chilli powder)

Curd (Indian style yoghurt)-1 table spoon

Cumin whole (*Jeera*)-1/2 tea spoon

Salt-1 level tea spoon (or to taste)

Tomato Ketchup-1 table spoon

Cooking oil-1 table spoon

Ghee (clarified butter)-1 tea spoon

Water-1 cup

Method using a pressure cooker

Blend together (in a blender preferably!) the onions, garlic, ginger and tomatoes to a fine paste.

Heat the oil in a pressure cooker.

Add cumin to the oil and as it turns brown, add this paste and gently fry the same.

As the paste starts giving off a nice aroma, add the soya granules and peas to it. Sauté gently.

Add all the dry condiments (masala), salt and curd to this mixture and keep stirring on low flame (SIM on a gas stove) till it starts becoming dry.

Add the Ketchup to the mixture and stir again.

At this juncture, add the *ghee* for a lovely flavour.

Add the water, close the lid with weight and bring it to full pressure on high flame i.e. when steam starts escaping from the vent (don't worry, you will hear that typical sound).

Switch off the heat source.

Let the cooker cool down on its own before opening it.

That's all. Your protein rich Soya *Mattar* is ready.

Method using a wok/deep sauce pan

Blend together (in a blender preferably!) the onions, garlic, ginger and tomatoes to a fine paste.

Heat the oil in a wok/pan.

Add cumin to the oil and as it turns brown, add this paste and gently fry the same.

As the paste starts giving off a nice aroma, add the soya granules and peas to it. Sauté gently.

Add all the dry condiments (masala), salt and curd to this mixture and keep stirring on low flame (SIM on a gas stove) till it starts becoming dry.

Add the Ketchup to the mixture and stir again.

At this juncture, add the *ghee* for a lovely flavour.

Add the water, and cover the wok/pan with a tight fitting lid and cook for about 15 minutes or till the soya granules are completely cooked.

Switch off the heat source.

That's all. Your protein rich Soya *Mattar* is ready.

Prep time: 7 minutes

Cooking time: 10 minutes with pressure cooker; 20 minutes with a wok/deep pan

Total time: 17 minutes with pressure cooker; 27 minutes with a wok/deep pan

Mushroom *Mattar* (Mushroom-Peas Curry)

A very popular North Indian curry that most restaurants would be happy to serve.

Serves 3-4

Ingredients

Mushroom (e.g. white snow button)—500 grams (2 cup)-cut into 1/2

Green peas (shelled, fresh are preferred) –1/2 cup (100 grams or 3.5 oz.)

Medium size Onions–2 (chopped)

Garlic-4 pieces

Ginger-1 inch (2.5 cm or 1/3rd length of a finger) piece

Fresh tomato-2 (chopped)

Turmeric (*Haldi*) - 1/2 tea spoon

Dry crushed coriander (*Dhania*) -2 tea spoon

Garam Masala (mixture of common Indian spices) crushed- 1/2 tea spoon

Tip: If you can't get ready-made *garam masala* mixture from a nearby Indian store, you can make yours by using 1 black cardamom, 3 green

cardamoms, 4 cloves, and 1 inch cinnamon-all ground together.

Kashmiri Red Chilli powder–1/4 tea spoon (Recommended for colour, but if you like your dish to be really spicy, use any other red chilli powder)

Curd (Indian style yoghurt)-1 table spoon

Cumin whole (*Jeera*)-1/2 tea spoon

Salt-1 level tea spoon (or to taste)

Tomato Ketchup-1 table spoon

Cooking oil-1 table spoon

Ghee (clarified butter)-1 tea spoon

Water-1 cup

Method using a pressure cooker

Blend together (in a blender preferably!) the onions, garlic, ginger and tomatoes to a fine paste.

Heat the oil in a pressure cooker.

Add cumin to the oil and as it turns brown, add this paste and gently fry the same.

As the paste starts giving off a nice aroma, add the mushroom and peas. Sauté gently.

Add all the dry condiments (masala), salt and curd to this mixture and keep stirring on low flame (SIM on a gas stove) till it starts becoming dry.

Add the Ketchup to the mixture and stir again.

At this juncture, add the *ghee* for a lovely flavour.

Add the water, close the lid with weight and bring it to full pressure on high flame i.e. when steam starts escaping from the vent (don't worry, you will hear that typical sound).

Switch off the heat source.

Let the cooker cool down on its own before opening it.

That's all. Your lovely Mushroom-*Mattar* Curry is ready.

Method using a wok/deep sauce pan

Blend together (in a blender preferably!) the onions, garlic, ginger and tomatoes to a fine paste.

Heat the oil in a wok/pan.

Add cumin to the oil and as it turns brown, add this paste and gently fry the same.

As the paste starts giving off a nice aroma, add the mushroom and peas to it. Sauté gently.

Add all the dry condiments (masala), salt and curd to this mixture and keep stirring on low flame (SIM on a gas stove) till it starts becoming dry.

Add the Ketchup to the mixture and stir again.

At this juncture, add the *ghee* for a lovely flavour.

Add the water, and cover the wok/pan with a tight fitting lid and cook for about 10 minutes or till the mushroom and peas are completely cooked.

Switch off the heat source.

That's all. Your lovely Mushroom-*Mattar* Curry is ready.

Prep time: 7 minutes

Cooking time: 10 minutes with pressure cooker; 15 minutes with a wok/deep pan

Total time: 17 minutes with pressure cooker; 22 minutes with a wok/deep pan

Phool Gobi, Chukander, Aloo, Mattar Sabzi (Cauliflower, Beetroot, Potatoes and Peas Curry)

Yet another lovely medley of seasonal vegetables made in the North Indian style.

Serves 3-4

Ingredients

Cauliflower–1/2 Kg (500 grams or 18oz or 2 cups)

Green peas (shelled, fresh are preferred)–200 grams (7oz) (1 cup)

Potatoes-2 (chopped)

Beetroot—1 (chopped)

Medium size Onions—2 (chopped)

Garlic-4 cloves

Ginger-1 inch

Fresh tomato-2 (chopped)

Turmeric (*Haldi*) powder- 1/2 tea spoon

Dry crushed coriander (*Dhania*) powder-2 tea spoon

Garam Masala (mixture of common Indian spices) crushed- 1/2 tea spoon

Tip: If you can't get ready-made *garam masala* mixture from a nearby Indian store, you can make yours by using 1 black cardamom, 3 green cardamoms, 4 cloves, and 1 inch cinnamon—all ground together.

Kashmiri Red Chilli powder–1/4 tea spoon (Recommended for colour, but if you like your dish to be really spicy, use some other red chilli powder)

Cumin (*Jeera*) whole-1/2 tea spoon

Salt-1 level tea spoon (or to taste)

Tomato Ketchup-1 table spoon

Cooking oil-1 table spoon

Ghee (clarified butter)-1 tea spoon

Water-1 tea cup

Method using a pressure cooker

Blend together (in a blender preferably!) the onions, garlic, ginger and tomatoes to a fine paste.

Heat the oil in a pressure cooker.

Add cumin to the oil and as it turns brown, add this paste and gently fry the same.

As the paste starts giving off a nice aroma, add all the vegetables (cauliflower, beet, peas and potatoes) and sauté gently.

Add all the dry condiments (masala) and salt to this mixture and keep stirring till all the vegetables are well coated.

Add the ketchup and *ghee* to the mixture and stir again.

Add the water, close the lid with weight and bring it to full pressure on high flame i.e. when steam starts escaping from the vent (don't worry, you will hear that typical sound).

Immediately turn off the heat source as otherwise your veggies will be overcooked.

Let the cooker cool down on its own before opening it.

That's all. Your *phoolgobi, chukander, aloo matter sabzi* (cauliflower, beetroot, peas and potatoes veggie curry) is ready.

Method using a wok/deep sauce pan

Blend together (in a blender preferably!) the onions, garlic, ginger and tomatoes to a fine paste.

Heat the oil in a wok/pan.

Add cumin to the oil and as it turns brown, add this paste and gently fry the same.

As the paste starts giving off a nice aroma, add all the vegetables (cauliflower, beet, peas and potatoes) and sauté gently.

Add all the dry condiments (masala) and salt to this mixture and keep stirring till all the vegetables are well coated.

Add the ketchup and *ghee* to the mixture and stir again.

Add the water, cover the wok/deep pan with a lid and reduce the heat to minimum. Let the vegetables cook to your liking for about 10 minutes. You may poke the vegetables once in a while with a fork to see whether they have been cooked.

Turn off the heat source as otherwise your veggies will be overcooked.

That's all. Your *phoolgobi, chukander, aloo matter sabzi* (cauliflower, beetroot, peas and potatoes veggie curry) is ready.

Prep time: 10 minutes

Cooking time: 7 minutes with pressure cooker; 15-20 minutes with a wok/deep pan

Total time: 17 minutes with pressure cooker; 25-30 minutes with a wok/deep pan

Paneer Makhni (Indian Cottage Cheese in a Rich Tomato Curry)

This is our vegetarian version of the popular Butter Chicken or the British Chicken Tikka Masala, except that we don't use any tandoor, *garam masala*, or even tear-jerking onions. The bright red curry is guaranteed to make this dish an instant hit with the young persons in your family.

Serves 3-4

Ingredients

Indian Cottage Cheese (*paneer*)–1/2 Kg (500 grams or 18oz or 2 cups); cut into bite size pieces

Chopped Tomatoes-3 large ripe

Tomato puree-200 grams (7oz) (1 cup)

Low fat fresh cream-200 grams (7oz) (1 cup)

Butter-1 tablespoon

Coriander (*Dhania*) powder-1 teaspoon

Cumin (*Jeera*) powder-1/2 teaspoon

Kashmiri Red Chilli powder–1/4 tea spoon (Recommended for colour, but if you like your dish to be really spicy, use some other red chilli powder)

Salt-1 teaspoon or to taste

Sugar-1 teaspoon

Cooking Oil-2 tablespoon

Cashew nuts-50 grams (2oz or 3 tablespoon), fried golden and then chopped.

(The method to fry the cashew nuts: in a small pan, add about a tablespoon of cooking oil. Put the pan on your heat source. When the oil heats up, add the cashew nuts and stir till they turn golden. Immediately remove the cashew nuts to a plate and chop. Remember, if you leave the cashew nuts in the pan, the hot oil will keep roasting the cashew nuts and may burn them.)

Method

Take a wok/deep sauce pan and put it on your heat source.

Add the cooking oil and let it warm up.

Now add the cottage cheese (*paneer*) pieces and gently roast till they become golden.

Remove the *paneer* pieces and keep aside.

Now add the butter to the wok/pan.

When the butter melts, add the coriander, cumin and the red chilli powder.

Let the mixture roast for 1 minute.

Add the tomatoes and cook till the tomatoes soften up.

Add the tomato puree, salt and sugar.

Gently keep stirring.

As the gravy turns a nice thick red colour, add the fresh low fat cream.

Stir well.

Now add the *paneer* pieces to the mixture and let it all come to a boil.

Reduce the heat and let the mixture simmer for about 2 minutes.

Switch off the heat source.

Sprinkle now the cashew nuts.

That's all. Your delicious *Paneer Makhni* is ready.

Prep time: 7 minutes

Cooking time: 10 minutes

Total time: 17 minutes

Paneer Kaju Curry (Indian Cottage Cheese with Cashew and Black Pepper)

This is a "white curry" dish, with NO chillies of any kind, which the young in your family may find just irresistible.

Serves 3-4

Ingredients

Indian Cottage Cheese (*paneer*)–1/2 Kg (500 grams or 18oz or 2 cups); cut into bite size pieces

Low fat fresh cream-400 grams (14oz) (2 cup)

Butter-1 tablespoon

Salt- ½ teaspoon or to taste

Sugar- ½ teaspoon

Cashew nuts- 1 cup (crushed)

Black Pepper- 1 tablespoon (crushed)

Cooking Oil–2 tablespoon

Method

Take a wok/deep sauce pan and put it on your heat source.

Add the cooking oil and let it warm up.

Now add the cottage cheese (*paneer*) pieces and gently roast till they become golden.

Remove the *paneer* pieces and keep aside.

Now add the butter to the wok/pan.

When the butter melts, add the crushed cashew nuts and roast for about two minutes.

Now add the fresh cream, salt, and sugar, and bring the mixture to a boil while stirring continuously.

Add the roasted *paneer* pieces and let the mixture again come to a boil.

Reduce the heat and let the mixture simmer for about 2 minutes.

Sprinkle the crushed black pepper.

Switch off the heat source.

That's all. Your delicious *Paneer Kaju* Curry is ready.

Prep time: 7 minutes

Cooking time: 10 minutes

Total time: 17 minutes

Paneer Kofta (Indian Cottage Cheese Balls in a Mild Coconut and Cream Curry)

This is a mild but really delicious curry. Try it once and again, the younger persons of your family will be hooked on for ever.

Serves 3-4

Ingredients

Indian Cottage Cheese (*paneer*)–1/2 Kg (500 grams or 18oz or 2 cups)

Onion-1 (chopped)

Garlic-4 cloves (large)

Ginger-1 inch

(Onion+ Garlic + Ginger to be made into a paste in a blender)

Garam Masala-1 teaspoon

Tip: If you can't get ready-made *garam masala* mixture from a nearby Indian store, you can make yours by using 1 black cardamom, 3 green cardamoms, 4 cloves, and 1 inch cinnamon–all ground together.

Kashmiri Red Chilli powder–1/4 tea spoon (Recommended for colour, but if you like your dish to be really spicy, use some other red chilli powder)

Green Chilli- 1 (deseeded and chopped)

Fresh Coriander (*Dhania*) leaves- chopped 3 tablespoon

Cumin Seeds (*Jeera*)-2 teaspoon

Cooking Oil-1 tablespoon (use a neutral oil and NOT one with strong flavour like mustard)

Desi Ghee (Clarified butter)-1 tablespoon

Coconut milk-200 ml (1 cup)

Low fat cream-200 ml (1 cup)

Salt- 1 and ½ teaspoon or to taste

Sugar- ½ teaspoon

Semolina (*Sooji*) - 1 tablespoon

Method

In a vessel, mix together the cottage cheese, ½ teaspoon cumin seeds, ½ teaspoon *garam masala*, green chillies, coriander leaves, *sooji*, ½ teaspoon salt and sugar.

Make egg shaped balls from this mixture and place them on a microwavable dish with some depth, as we will be adding curry to this mixture. Keep some space between the balls as they tend to swell up.

Place the wok/deep sauce pan on your heat source.

Add the cooking oil and when it warms up, add the *desi ghee* and the cumin seeds.

The moment the cumin seeds start browning, add the (onion + garlic + ginger) paste.

Gently stir the mixture and as the mixture starts to brown, add the remaining *garam masala*, salt (to taste) and the red chilli powder for the curry.

Keep stirring and when the oil separates from the mixture, add the coconut milk and the low fat cream and mix well.

Remove from fire.

Pour this mixture over the balls and microwave for 5 minutes,

That's all. Your *Paneer Koftas* are ready.

Prep Time: 10 minutes

Cooking Time: 10 minutes

Total Time: 20 minutes

Lauki Aloo (Bottle Gourd Potato Curry)

This is a simple dish made in the North Indian style. Bottle gourd would have never tasted so wonderful, I swear.

Serves 3-4

Ingredients

Bottle Gourd— 1 (peeled and chopped into 2" pieces)

Potato (peeled and chopped into bite size pieces) – 250 grams (1 cup)

Medium size Onions–2 (chopped)

Garlic-4 cloves

Ginger-1 inch (2.5 cm or 1/3rd length of a finger) piece

Fresh tomato-2 (chopped)

Turmeric (*Haldi*) - 1/2 tea spoon

Dry crushed coriander (*Dhania*)-2 tea spoon

Garam Masala (mixture of common Indian spices) crushed- 1/2 tea spoon

Tip: If you can't get ready-made *garam masala* mixture from a nearby Indian store, you can make yours by using 1 black cardamom, 3 green

cardamoms, 4 cloves, and 1 inch cinnamon–all ground together.

Kashmiri Red Chilli powder–1/4 tea spoon (Recommended for colour, but if you like your dish to be really spicy, use any other red chilli powder)

Cumin whole (*Jeera*)-1/2 tea spoon

Salt-1 level tea spoon (or to taste)

Tomato Ketchup-1 table spoon

Cooking oil-1 table spoon

Ghee (clarified butter)-1 tea spoon

Water-1 cup

Method using a pressure cooker

Blend together (in a blender preferably!) the onions, garlic, ginger and tomatoes to a fine paste.

Heat the oil in a pressure cooker.

Add cumin to the oil and as it turns brown, add this paste and gently fry the same.

As the paste starts giving off a nice aroma, add the bottle gourd and potato pieces to it. Sauté gently.

Add all the dry condiments (masala) and salt to this mixture and keep stirring on low flame (SIM on a gas stove) till it starts becoming dry.

Add the ketchup to the mixture and stir again.

At this juncture, add the *ghee* for a lovely flavour.

Add the water, close the lid with weight and bring it to full pressure on high flame i.e. when steam starts escaping from the vent (don't worry, you will hear that typical sound).

Switch off the heat source.

Let the cooker cool down on its own before opening it.

That's all. Your delicious *Lauki Aloo* is ready.

Method using a wok/deep sauce pan

Blend together (in a blender preferably!) the onions, garlic, ginger and tomatoes to a fine paste.

Heat the oil in a wok/pan.

Add cumin to the oil and as it turns brown, add this paste and gently fry the same.

As the paste starts giving off a nice aroma, add the bottle gourd and potato pieces to it. Sauté gently.

Add all the dry condiments (masala) and salt to this mixture and keep stirring on low flame (SIM on a gas stove) till it starts becoming dry.

Add the ketchup to the mixture and stir again.

At this juncture, add the *ghee* for a lovely flavour.

Add the water, cover the wok/pan with a tight fitting lid and cook for about 15 minutes or till the potatoes are completely cooked.

Switch off the heat source.

That's all. Your delicious *Lauki Aloo* is ready.

Prep time: 7 minutes

Cooking time: 10 minutes with pressure cooker; 20 minutes with a wok/deep pan

Total time: 17 minutes with pressure cooker; 27 minutes with a wok/deep pan

Bean Potato Curry

Yet another North/East Indian dish that uplifts the humble French Beans to almost gourmet level.

Serves 3-4

Ingredients

Fresh French Beans—500 grams (2 cup)-cut into 2" pieces

Potato (peeled and chopped in to bite size pieces)– 250 grams (1 cup)

Medium size Onions–2 (chopped)

Garlic-4 pieces

Ginger-1 inch (2.5 cm or 1/3rd length of a finger) piece

Fresh tomato-2 (chopped)

Turmeric (*Haldi*) - 1/2 tea spoon

Dry crushed coriander (*Dhania*)-2 tea spoon

Garam Masala (mixture of common Indian spices) crushed- 1/2 tea spoon

Tip: If you can't get ready-made *garam masala* mixture from a nearby Indian store, you can make yours by using 1 black cardamom, 3 green

cardamoms, 4 cloves, and 1 inch cinnamon—all ground together.

Kashmiri Red Chilli powder–1/4 tea spoon (Recommended for colour, but if you like your dish to be really spicy, use any other red chilli powder)

Cumin whole (*Jeera*)-1/2 tea spoon

Salt-1 level tea spoon or to taste

Tomato Ketchup-1 table spoon

Cooking oil-1 table spoon

Ghee (clarified butter)-1 tea spoon

Water-1 cup

Method using a pressure cooker

Blend together (in a blender preferably!) the onions, garlic, ginger and tomatoes to a fine paste.

Heat the oil in a pressure cooker.

Add cumin to the oil and as it turns brown, add this paste and gently fry the same.

As the paste starts giving off a nice aroma, add the beans and potato to it. Sauté gently.

Add all the dry condiments (masala) and salt to this mixture and keep stirring on low flame (SIM on a gas stove) till it starts becoming dry.

Add the ketchup to the mixture and stir again.

At this juncture, add the *ghee* for a lovely flavour.

Add the water, close the lid with weight and bring it to full pressure on high flame i.e. when steam starts escaping from the vent (don't worry, you will hear that typical sound).

Switch off the heat source.

Let the cooker cool down on its own before opening it.

That's all. Your simple Bean *Aloo* dish is ready.

Method using a wok/deep sauce pan

Blend together (in a blender preferably!) the onions, garlic, ginger and tomatoes to a fine paste.

Heat the oil in a wok/pan.

Add cumin to the oil and as it turns brown, add this paste and gently fry the same.

As the paste starts giving off a nice aroma, add the beans and potato to it. Sauté gently.

Add all the dry condiments (masala) and salt to this mixture and keep stirring on low flame (SIM on a gas stove) till it starts becoming dry.

Add the ketchup to the mixture and stir again.

At this juncture, add the *ghee* for a lovely flavour.

Add the water, cover the wok/pan with a tight fitting lid and cook for about 15 minutes or till the beans and potatoes are completely cooked.

Switch off the heat source.

That's all. Your simple but tasty Bean *Aloo* dish is ready.

Prep time: 7 minutes

Cooking time: 10 minutes with pressure cooker; 20 minutes with a wok/deep pan

Total time: 17 minutes with pressure cooker; 27 minutes with a wok/deep pan

Lauki-Chana Dal (Bottle Gourd and Split Chick Pea)

This is a great Bengali (Eastern Indian) dish that infuses the proteins of lentils in a humble vegetable in a really delicious manner.

Serves 3-4

Ingredients

Chana Dal (split chick pea)-1/2 cup

Water-4 cups (same cup as above!)

Bottle Gourd— 1 (peeled and chopped into 2" pieces)

Turmeric (*Haldi*) powder-1/2 tea spoon

Salt–1/2 tea spoon or to taste

Tomato—2 (chopped)

Onion-1 (chopped)

Garlic-2 pieces (chopped)

Ginger-1 inch (chopped)

Cumin seeds (*Jeera*)–1/2 tea spoon

Garam Masala (mixture of common Indian spices) crushed- 1/2 tea spoon

Tip: If you can't get ready-made *garam masala* mixture from a nearby Indian store, you can make yours by using 1 black cardamom, 3 green cardamoms, 4 cloves, and 1 inch cinnamon–all ground together.

Ghee (clarified butter)-2 table spoon

Method using a pressure cooker

Wash the *chana* dal well.

Put the pressure cooker on your heat source and add *ghee* (clarified butter).

When the *ghee* heats up, add the cumin seeds and let these brown.

Add the chopped onion, garlic and ginger. Sauté for 2 minutes.

Add the bottle gourd and the tomatoes and sauté for another minute.

Add the *chana* dal, turmeric, salt, and water and *garam masala*.

Close the lid and let it come to full pressure on high flame i.e. when steam starts escaping from the vent (don't worry, you will hear that typical sound).

Reduce heat (to Sim on a gas stove) and let it cook for 10 more minutes.

Turn off the heat source and let the cooker cool down.

That's all. Your simple *Lauki-Chana Dal* is ready.

Method using a wok/deep sauce pan

Pre-soak the *chana dal* for at least four hours.

Put the wok/pan on your heat source and add *ghee* (clarified butter).

When the *ghee* heats up, add the cumin seeds and let these brown.

Add the chopped onion, garlic and ginger. Sauté for 2 minutes.

Add the bottle gourd and the tomatoes and sauté for another minute.

Add the *chana* dal, turmeric, salt, water and *garam masala*.

Reduce heat (to Sim on a gas stove) and let it cook for about 40 minutes or till the *chana* dal is fully cooked.

Turn off the heat source.

That's all. Your simple *Lauki-Chana Dal* is ready.

Prep time: 7 minutes (excluding pre-soak time)

Cooking time: 15 minutes with pressure cooker; 45 minutes with a wok/deep pan

Total time: 22 minutes with pressure cooker; 52 minutes with a wok/deep pan

Parwal Dorma (Pointed Gourd in an Exotic Curry)

Bristling with the goodness of coconut, cashew, poppy seeds and so many Indian spices, this is a quite a gourmet dish from Eastern India. *Parwal* would never taste so great, I guarantee.

Serves 3-4

Ingredients

Parwal- 500 grams (2 cups)

Onion-1 (large, chopped)

Ginger- 1 inch chopped

Garlic- 6 cloves chopped

(Onion+ Ginger+ Garlic made in to a fine paste in a blender)

Turmeric (*Haldi*)-1/2 tea spoon

Coriander (*Dhania*) powder- 1 teaspoon

Kashmiri Red Chilli powder–1/4 tea spoon (Recommended for colour, but if you like your dish to be really spicy, use some other red chilli powder)

Cumin (*Jeera*) seeds- 1 teaspoon

Garam Masala (mixture of common Indian spices) crushed- 1/2 teaspoon

Tip: If you can't get ready-made *garam masala* mixture from a nearby Indian store, you can make yours by using 1 black cardamom, 3 green cardamoms, 4 cloves, and 1 inch cinnamon—all ground together.

Tomato puree- 200 grams (1 cup)

Cashew nuts - 2 table spoon

Poppy seeds (*khas khas*) - 2 table spoon

(Cashew + poppy seeds to be ground dry in a hard spice grinder)

Desiccated coconut powder- 2 table spoon

Salt-1 tea spoon (or to taste)

Sugar- ½ teaspoon

Cooking Oil- ½ cup

Water- 2 cups

Method

Scratch (not peel) the surface of the *parwals* and wash well.

Now slit each *parwal* in to 2 pieces lengthwise.

In a wok or deep sauce pan, add the cooking oil, and place it on your heat source.

As the oil heats up, add the *parwal* and gently fry till golden. Keep aside.

Switch off the heat source.

Leaving about three table spoon of oil in the wok, pour out rest of the oil in a dry container. This can be used for some other dish.

Be careful as the oil would be very hot.

Switch on the heat source again and put the wok on it with just three table spoon oil.

As the oil heats up, add the cumin seeds.

As soon as the cumin seeds turn brown, which takes just a few seconds (do please make sure they don't burn), add the onion, garlic and ginger paste.

Sauté well till the paste starts giving a nice aroma.

Now add the chilli powder, turmeric powder, *garam masala*, coriander powder, salt and sugar.

Sauté till the mixture turns a light brown colour.

Now add the ground cashew nut, poppy seeds and the desiccated coconut powder. Stir well.

To this mixture, add the tomato puree.

Stir till the mixture dries up somewhat.

Add the water and the fried *parwal*.

Let the mixture come to a boil.

Reduce the heat and cook the curry for five minutes more.

Switch off the heat source.

That's all. Your gourmet *parwal dorma* is ready.

Prep time: 10 minutes

Cooking time: 25 minutes

Total time: 35 minutes

Lauki Kofta (Bottle Gourd Balls in Curry)

This is just that gourmet dish for those special occasions. Your guests will find it difficult to believe that you used the humble bottle gourd to come up with this mouth-watering concoction.

Serves 3-4

Ingredients

Bottle Gourd— 1 (peeled and grated)

Split Chick-pea flour (*Besan*) - ½ cup (125 grams)

Medium size Onions–2 (chopped)

Garlic-4 pieces (chopped)

Ginger-1 inch (2.5 cm or 1/3rd length of a finger, chopped)

Fresh tomato-2 (chopped)

Turmeric (*Haldi*) - 1 tea spoon

Dry crushed coriander (*Dhania*)-3 tea spoon

Garam Masala (mixture of common Indian spices) crushed- 1/2 tea spoon

Tip: If you can't get ready-made *garam masala* mixture from a nearby Indian store, you can make yours by using 1 black cardamom, 3 green

cardamoms, 4 cloves, and 1 inch cinnamon–all ground together.

Kashmiri Red Chilli powder–1 tea spoon (Recommended for colour, but if you like your dish to be really spicy, use any other red chilli powder)

Cumin whole (*Jeera*)-1 tea spoon

Asafoetida (*Hing*) - ½ teaspoon

Tomato Ketchup-1 table spoon

Salt-1 and 1/2 tea spoon or to taste

Cooking oil- enough to deep fry

Ghee (clarified butter)-1 tea spoon

Water-2 cup

Method for Koftas

Mix together the grated bottle gourd, *besan*, ½ teaspoon turmeric, 1 teaspoon coriander powder, ½ teaspoon red chilli powder, ½ teaspoon salt and ½ teaspoon asafoetida (*hing*).

Set aside for 15 minutes and then make into egg-sized balls.

Heat oil in a wok/deep sauce pan and deep fry these balls. Keep aside these *koftas*.

Method for the curry

Blend together (in a blender preferably!) the onions, garlic, ginger and tomatoes to a fine paste.

Heat 1 tablespoon oil in another wok/deep sauce pan.

Tip: You can use the same oil that you used for frying the *koftas*.

Add cumin to the oil and as it turns brown, add the onion-ginger-garlic-tomato paste and gently fry.

As the paste starts giving off a nice aroma, add all the remaining dry condiments (masala) and salt to this mixture and keep stirring on low flame (SIM on a gas stove) till it starts becoming dry.

Add the ketchup to the mixture and stir again. At this juncture, add the *ghee* for a lovely flavour. Add the water, and bring the mixture to a boil on high flame.

Gently add the fried *koftas* to this curry and reduce the flame.

Let these cook for 5 minutes.

Switch off the heat source.

Prep time: 10 minutes (excluding time for the *kofta* batter to set)

Cooking time: 20 minutes

Total time: 30 minutes

Aloo Mattar (Potato-Peas Curry)

This is again a very popular dish that with some variation you will find at every wayside eatery (dhaba), especially in North India in the winters when peas are available in plenty.

Serves 3-4

Ingredients

Potato (peeled and chopped in to bite size pieces)– 500 grams (2 cup)

Green peas (de-shelled, fresh are preferred)–1/2 cup

Medium size Onions–2 (chopped)

Garlic-4 pieces (chopped)

Ginger-1 inch (2.5 cm or 1/3rd length of a finger) piece (chopped)

Fresh tomato-2 (chopped)

Turmeric (*Haldi*)- 1/2 tea spoon

Dry crushed coriander (*Dhania*)-2 tea spoon

Garam Masala (mixture of common Indian spices) crushed- 1/2 tea spoon

Tip: If you can't get ready-made *garam masala* mixture from a nearby Indian store, you can make yours by using 1 black cardamom, 3 green

cardamoms, 4 cloves, and 1 inch cinnamon—all ground together.

Kashmiri Red Chilli powder–1/4 tea spoon (Recommended for colour, but if you like your dish to be really spicy, use any other red chilli powder)

Cumin whole (*Jeera*)-1/2 tea spoon

Salt-1 level tea spoon (or to taste)

Tomato Ketchup-1 table spoon

Cooking oil-1 table spoon

Ghee (clarified butter)-1 tea spoon

Water-1 cup

Method using a pressure cooker

Heat the oil in a pressure cooker.

Add cumin to the oil and as it turns brown, add the chopped onion, garlic, and ginger.

Gently fry the same till it starts giving off a nice aroma.

Now add the potato and peas. Sauté gently.

Add all the dry condiments (masala) and salt to this mixture and keep stirring on low flame (SIM on a gas stove) till it starts becoming dry.

Add the ketchup and the tomatoes to the mixture and stir again.

At this juncture, add the *ghee* for a lovely flavour.

Stir till the tomatoes are cooked.

Add the water, close the lid with weight and bring it to full pressure on high flame i.e. when steam starts escaping from the vent (don't worry, you will hear that typical sound).

Switch off the heat source.

Let the cooker cool down on its own before opening it.

That's all. Your simple *Aloo-Mattar* Curry is ready.

Method using a wok/deep sauce pan

Heat the oil in a wok/pan.

Add cumin to the oil and as it turns brown, add the chopped onion, garlic, and ginger.

Gently fry the same till it starts giving off a nice aroma.

Now add the potato and peas. Sauté gently.

Add all the dry condiments (masala) and salt to this mixture and keep stirring on low flame (SIM on a gas stove) till it starts becoming dry.

Add the ketchup and the tomatoes to the mixture and stir again.

At this juncture, add the *ghee* for a lovely flavour.

Stir till the tomatoes are cooked.

Add the water, cover the wok/pan with a tight fitting lid and cook for about 10 minutes or till the potatoes and peas are completely cooked.

Switch off the heat source.

That's all. Your simple *Aloo-Mattar Curry* is ready.

Prep time: 7 minutes

Cooking time: 10 minutes with pressure cooker; 15 minutes with a wok/deep pan

Total time: 17 minutes with pressure cooker; 22 minutes with a wok/deep pan

Gatta Curry (Chick Pea Flour Patties in Curry)

This is a Western Indian dish, from the deserts of Rajasthan, where in the absence of fresh greens you are forced to make do with just chick pea flour. But you have to doff your hat to the Rajasthanis for coming up with such a delicious curry even in such difficult circumstances.

Serves 3-4

Ingredients

Split Chick-pea flour (*Besan*) - 1 cup (250 grams)

Medium size Onions–2 (chopped)

Garlic-4 pieces (chopped)

Ginger-1 inch (2.5 cm or 1/3rd length of a finger) piece (chopped)

Fresh tomato-2 (chopped)

Turmeric (*Haldi*) - 1 tea spoon

Dry crushed coriander (*Dhania*)-3 tea spoon

Garam Masala (mixture of common Indian spices) crushed- 1/2 tea spoon

Tip: If you can't get ready-made *garam masala* mixture from a nearby Indian store, you can make yours by using 1 black cardamom, 3 green

cardamoms, 4 cloves, and 1 inch cinnamon–all ground together.

Kashmiri Red Chilli powder–1 tea spoon (Recommended for colour, but if you like your dish to be really spicy, use any other red chilli powder)

Cumin whole (*Jeera*)-1 tea spoon

Asafoetida (*Hing*) - ½ teaspoon

Tomato Ketchup-1 table spoon

Salt-1 and 1/2 tea spoon (or to taste)

Cooking oil- enough to deep fry

Ghee (clarified butter)-1 tea spoon

Water-2 and 1/2 cup

Method for making the Gatta

Mix together the *besan*, ½ teaspoon turmeric, 1 teaspoon coriander powder, ½ teaspoon red chilli powder, ½ teaspoon salt and ½ teaspoon asafoetida (*hing*) with ½ a cup of water.

Set aside for 15 minutes.

Take the mixture in your hands and make 6" long sausage shaped patties.

In a muslin cloth, place all these patties, and tie a knot.

In a pan put two cups of water and bring it to a boil.

Place the muslin cloth with the patties in the boiling water and cook for 5 minutes.

Remove the patties from the water and let them cool down.

Tip: You can retain this water for use in the curry later.

With a knife, cut the patties in to 1" round pieces and keep aside.

Heat oil in a wok/deep sauce pan and deep fry these round patties till they turn a nice golden brown.

Take out on a plate.

Keep aside.

Method for the curry

Blend together (in a blender preferably!) the onions, garlic, ginger and tomatoes to a fine paste.

Heat 1 tablespoon oil in another wok/deep sauce pan.

Tip: You can use the same oil that you used for frying the *gattas.*

Add cumin to the oil and as it turns brown, add the onion-ginger-garlic-tomato paste and gently fry.

As the paste starts giving off a nice aroma, add all the remaining dry masala and salt to this mixture and keep stirring on low flame (SIM on a gas stove) till it starts becoming dry.

Add the Ketchup to the mixture and stir again.

At this juncture, add the *ghee* for a lovely flavour.

Add the water (you can use the same water that you boiled the *gattas* in), and bring it to a boil on high flame.

Gently add the fried *gattas* to this curry and reduce the flame.

Let these cook for 2 minutes.

Switch off the heat source.

That's all. Your delicious Rajasthani *Gatta* Curry is ready.

Prep time: 10 minutes

Cooking time: 20 minutes

Total time: 30 minutes

***Dhokha* Curry (Chick Pea Flour Patties Curry)**

This is a Bihari (Eastern Indian) variation of the Rajasthani *Gattas*. Because in taste it mimics the popular fish fry, the locals call it *Dhokha* or deception!

Serves 3-4

Ingredients for dhokhas

Split Chick-pea flour (*Besan*)-2 cup (500 grams)

Turmeric (*Haldi*) –1/2 tea spoon

Dry crushed coriander (*Dhania*)-1 tea spoon

Kashmiri Red Chilli powder—1/2 tea spoon (Recommended for colour, but if you like your dish to be really spicy, use any other red chilli powder)

Asafoetida (*Hing*) - ½ teaspoon

Garlic- 8 cloves (crushed)

Mustard Paste- 2 tablespoon

Salt- 1 tea spoon (or to taste)

Cooking oil- enough to deep fry

Water-1 cup

Ingredients for the curry

Fenugreek (*Methi*) seeds- ½ teaspoon

Garlic- 8 cloves (crushed)

Mustard Paste- 2 tablespoon

Tomatoes- 2 (chopped)

Tomato paste- 2 tablespoon

Salt- 1 tea spoon (or to taste)

Cooking oil- 2 tablespoon

Water-1 cup

Method for making dhokhas

Mix together all the ingredients for making the *dhokhas*, along with the water, EXCEPT for the cooking oil.

Set aside for 15 minutes.

Place a wok/deep sauce pan on your heat source and add 1 tablespoon of cooking oil.

As soon as the oil heats up, add this *dhokha* mixture and keep stirring till the mixture becomes dry.

Remove to a plate and flatten it. Allow this to cool down.

Cut rectangular pieces.

Heat oil in a wok/deep sauce pan and deep fry these rectangular pieces till they turn a nice golden brown.

Take out on a plate. Keep aside.

Note: You can serve these as snacks at this stage, unless you want to have a curry.

Method for making the curry

Heat 2 tablespoon oil in another wok/deep sauce pan.

(You can use the same oil that you used for frying the *dhokhas*.)

Add fenugreek seeds to the oil and as these turn brown, add the garlic and gently fry.

Now add the mustard, tomatoes, tomato paste and salt to this mixture.

Keep stirring on low flame (SIM on a gas stove) till the tomatoes are cooked.

Add the water and bring it to a boil on high flame.

Gently add the fried *dhokhas* to this curry and reduce the flame.

Let these cook for 2 minutes.

Switch off the heat source.

That's all. Your mouth-watering Bihari *Dhokha* Curry is ready.

Prep time: 15 minutes

Cooking time: 20 minutes

Total time: 35 minutes

Split Urad Dal (Black Lentils) with Spinach

This is a great Bengali (Eastern Indian) dish that once again infuses the proteins from lentils into the humble spinach in an intriguing but delicious twist.

Serves 3-4

Ingredients

Split *Urad Dal*- 1/2 cup

Water-3 cups

Spinach- 2 cups (washed and chopped)

Ginger-1 inch (2.5 cm or 1/3rd length of a finger) piece

Cumin (*Jeera*) seeds- ½ tea spoon

Fresh tomatoes-3 (washed and chopped)

Ghee (clarified butter) - 1 table spoon

Salt-to taste (or 1 level teaspoon roughly)

Method using a pressure cooker

In a pan, dry roast the *urad dal* till it turns a nice golden brown colour.

Now wash this dal and keep aside.

In a pressure cooker, add the *ghee* and put it on your heat source.

As soon as the *ghee* melts, add the cumin seeds and ginger.

As soon as the cumin seeds brown, add the spinach and the tomatoes.

Stir well.

Now add the *urad dal*, salt, and water.

Close the lid of the cooker with weight.

Once it comes to full pressure, (i.e. when the weight lifts and there is a whistling sound), turn down the flame (to SIM on a gas stove) and let it cook for 15 minutes.

Switch off the heat source and once the cooker cools down, take out the dal.

That's all. Your *urad-spinach* dal is ready.

Method using a wok/deep sauce pan

In a wok/pan, dry roast the *urad dal* till it turns a nice golden brown colour.

Now wash this dal and keep aside.

In the wok/pan, add the *ghee* and put it back on your heat source.

As soon as the *ghee* melts, add the cumin seeds and ginger.

As soon as the cumin seeds brown, add the spinach and the tomatoes.

Stir well.

Now add the *urad* dal, salt, and water.

Add the water, cover the wok/deep pan with a lid and reduce the heat to minimum. Let the *urad* dal cook to your liking for about 30 minutes.

Switch off the heat source.

That's all. Your *urad*-spinach dal is ready.

Prep time: 7 minutes

Cooking time: 15 minutes with pressure cooker; 40 minutes with a wok/pan

Total time: 22 minutes with pressure cooker; 47 minutes with a wok/pan

Chapter 4: Veggies Cooked with Rice and Breads

"The more colourful the food, the better. I try to add colour to my diet, which means vegetables and fruits."

–Misty May-Treanor

Trust the Indian ingenuity to infuse the goodness of veggies in to the humdrum rice and breads.

To be sure, from time immemorial, almost every cuisine that came into contact with Indian cooking was charmed into incorporating veggies and lentils into its food. For example, when the Zoroastrian Parsis first fled to India, in the 7th and 8th centuries, they encountered dal which was not a staple in their native Iran. So they invented their own unique dishes that had chunks of meat made with lentils resulting into the famous *dhansaak*.

The Mughals were equally enthusiastic in experimenting with dal, which they were otherwise unfamiliar with in Samarkand, or wherever they came from in Uzbekistan. As Vir Sanghvi postulates:

"In the 16th and 17th centuries, the staple food of Indian peasants was kitchdi, made with dal and rice (or sometimes, millets). The Mughals who were used to the pulaos of Central Asia, were unfamiliar with the idea of cooking rice with dal. They fell in love with kitchdi and in the 15 years that Humayun spent in exile, his Indian cooks made kitchdi for his guests including the Shah of Iran. Jehangir was so fond of Gujarati kitchdi that he ate it regularly in his palace."

A similar experiment took place when veggies were infused in to the Afghan Naan bread, and upgraded to the Indian stuffed *parathas*.

I, therefore, start by cataloguing my "Home Style versions" of ten outstanding ways to infuse your rice and Indian breads with veggies: five combo dishes of rice cooked with veggies and five stuffed *parathas*.

Khichdi (Mixture Dish of Rice, Lentil and Veggies)

Khichdi literally means a mixture. In some form or another, this is almost compulsorily prepared for the festival of *Makar Sakranti* that is celebrated all over India and Nepal. This festival is also known as *Pongal* in Tamil Nadu, *Bihu* in Assam, *Lohri* in Punjab or *Uttarayan* in Gujarat.

Interestingly, this is one of the few Hindu festivals that falls on the fixed day of 14 January, when the Sun moves from the Tropic of Capricorn to the Tropic of Cancer heralding the arrival of spring and the beginning of the harvest season.

It is believed that on this day, Lord *Surya* (the Sun God) visits the house of his son *Shani* (Saturn), who is the lord of the *Makar rashi* (Capricorn) and the controller of the quantum of misfortune befalling humans. To appease *Shani*, therefore, many Indians prefer cooking *Khichdi* on Saturdays which is also known as *Shaniwar* or the day of Lord *Shani*.

Khichdi is otherwise the most nutritionally complete dish, consisting of carbs from rice, proteins from lentils and vitamins from veggies. Also it is quite a JIFFY dish.

Ingredients

Rice-3/4 cup

Moong Dal (Bengal Gram)-1/4 cup

Onion-1 (chopped up)

Ginger-1 inch (2.5 cm or 1/3rd length of a finger) piece

Spinach (only leaves)-500 grams or 18oz or 2 cups coarsely chopped

Peas–100 grams (half cup) (3.5oz)

Carrots-2 (cut into small pieces)

Tomato-1

Khada (that is, whole and not powdered) *Garam Masala* (Green cardamom-2, brown cardamom-1, Bay leaves-2, cinnamon stick-1/2 inch, black pepper-6, cloves-4, cumin seeds-1/2 tea spoon)

Coriander (*Dhania*) powder-1 teaspoon

Red chilli powder (only for flavour and not to make it hot)-1/4 teaspoon (you can add more if you like it hot)

Turmeric (*Haldi*) powder-1 teaspoon

Asafoetida (*Hing*)-1/4 teaspoon

Ghee (clarified butter)-2 tablespoon full

Salt- 1 level teaspoon or to taste

Water-3 cups (This will give your *Khichdi* a wet consistency. However, if you like your *Khichdi* to be drier, then add only 2 cups of water instead of 3.)

Method

Wash the rice and dal together and let it dry for 5 minutes on an inclined plate.

If using a pressure cooker:

In a pressure cooker, put the clarified butter and put it on your heat source.

As it warms up, add the *Khada Garam Masala* and Asafoetida.

Let these all crackle but NOT burn.

Now add the onion and ginger.

Sauté this for 2 minutes and then add the peas and the carrots.

Stir well.

Now add the coarsely chopped spinach, turmeric, coriander powder, red chilli powder and salt.

Add the rice, dal and the tomatoes.

Stir well.

Add the water and put the lid with the weight on the cooker.

After the cooker comes to full pressure, i.e. when steam starts escaping from the vent (don't worry, you will hear that typical sound), switch off the heat source but do NOT release the pressure.

Let the pressure cooker cool down by itself.

Open the cooker and you will find your *Khichdi* ready.

If using a thick bottomed pan/vessel:

In a pan/vessel, add the clarified butter and place it on your heat source.

When the butter warms up, add the *Khada Garam Masala* and Asafoetida (*Hing*).

Let these all crackle but NOT burn.

Now add the onion and ginger.

Sauté this for 2 minutes.

Then add the peas and the carrots.

Stir well.

Then add the coarsely chopped spinach, turmeric, coriander powder, red chilli powder and salt.

Add the rice, dal and the tomatoes.

Stir well.

Add the water.

Cover the pan/vessel with a well-fitting lid.

Reduce the heat to minimum.

In other words, if cooking on gas, turn the knob to SIM (mer).

Let the *Khichdi* cook for 15-20 minutes.

Switch off the heat source and let the rice remain in the vessel for another 5 minutes.

Your *Khichdi* should now be ready.

Prep time: 5 minutes

Cooking time: 10 minutes with a pressure cooker; 20-25 minutes with a deep pan

Total time: 15 minutes with a pressure cooker; 25-30 minutes with a deep pan

Mattar Pulao (Peas Rice)

This is a simple rice dish that really goes well with any curry.

Ingredients

Long grain rice (Basmati)-1 cup

Water-2 cups (the same cup please as used for measuring the rice)

Peas-1/2 cup

Sliced Onion-1 (Medium)

Cumin seeds (*Jeera*)-1/2 teaspoon

Green Cardamom (*Chhoti elaichi*)-2

Cinnamon (*Dalchini*)-1/2 inch

Cloves (*Laung*)-4

Bay leaf (*Tejpatta*)-1

Clarified butter (*Ghee*)-2 tablespoon

Salt- 1 level teaspoon or to taste

Sugar-1/4 teaspoon

Method

Wash the rice well (in a vessel 3-4 times, but don't rub it lest the grains break) and let it naturally "dry", on an inclined plate, for 15-20 minutes. This helps enhance the aroma.

If using a pressure cooker:

In a pressure cooker, add the clarified butter and place it on your heat source.

When the butter warms up, add the cumin seeds along with the cardamom, cinnamon, cloves and bay leaves.

As soon as it starts giving a nice aroma, in less than a minute, add the onion slices and fry till translucent. Do please make sure that the spices brown and not burn, otherwise your dish will be totally spoiled.

Add the peas and stir for a minute.

Now add the rice along with the salt and sugar.

Stir well.

Add the water.

Close the lid of the pressure cooker BUT remove the weight.

When steam starts escaping from the vent (don't worry, you will hear that typical sound), reduce the heat to minimum. In other words, if cooking on gas, turn the knob to SIM (mer).

Wait for 10 minutes and switch off the gas.

Take out the rice.

Your pea *pulao* is ready.

If using a thick bottomed pan/vessel:

In a pan/vessel, add the clarified butter and place on fire.

When the butter warms up, add the cumin seeds along with the cardamom, cinnamon, cloves and bay leaves.

As soon as it starts giving a nice aroma, in less than a minute, add the onion slices and fry till translucent. Do please make sure that the spices brown and not burn, otherwise your dish will be totally spoiled.

Add the peas and stir for a minute.

Now add the rice along with the salt and sugar.

Stir well.

Add the water.

Cover the pan/vessel with a well-fitting lid.

Reduce the heat to minimum. In other words, if cooking on gas, turn the knob to SIM (mer).

Let the rice cook for 15-20 minutes.

Switch off the heat source and let the rice remain in the vessel for another 5 minutes.

Take out the rice.

Your pea *pulao* is ready.

If using a rice cooker:

In a pan/vessel, add the clarified butter and place on fire.

When the butter warms up, add the cumin seeds along with the cardamom, cinnamon, cloves and bay leaves.

As soon as it starts giving a nice aroma, in less than a minute, add the onion slices and fry till translucent. Do please make sure that the spices brown and not burn, otherwise your dish will be totally spoiled.

Add the peas and stir for a minute.

Now add the rice along with the salt and sugar.

Stir well.

Switch off the heat source and put all the ingredients into the rice cooker.

Add water.

Switch on the rice cooker and the let the rice cook. The rice cooker will switch off on its own when the rice is cooked.

Prep time: 20 minutes

Cooking time: 12 minutes with a pressure cooker; 17-22 minutes with a deep pan; and as indicated in the rice cooker manual

Total time: 32 minutes with a pressure cooker; 37-42 minutes with a deep pan

Mixed Vegetable Cheese *Biryani*

Who says vegetarians can't enjoy *Biryanis*? Try this dish and I guarantee you the same flavours as of any normal non-vegetarian *Biryani* and almost the same protein levels too (that are brought in by the tofu or *paneer*).

Ingredients

Long grain rice (Basmati)-2 cups

Cottage Cheese (*Paneer*) or *Tofu*-200 grams (7oz) (1 cup)

Peas-1/4 cup

Carrots cut into small pieces-1/4 cup

Cauliflower florets-1/4 cup

Beans-1/4 cup

Blanched Almonds-2 tablespoon

(To blanch almonds, immerse them in half a cup of hot water for 30 minutes. Remove the skin thereafter.)

Sliced Onion-1 (Medium)

Chopped Ginger-1 inch piece

Chopped Garlic-4 cloves

Turmeric (*Haldi*) powder-1/2 teaspoon

Red chilli powder (only for flavour and not to make it hot)-1/4 teaspoon (you can add more if you like it hot)

Coriander (*Dhania*) powder-1 teaspoon

Garam Masala (mixture of common Indian spices) - 1/2 teaspoon

Tip: If you can't get ready-made *garam masala* mixture from a nearby Indian store, you can make yours by using 1 black cardamom, 3 green cardamoms, 4 cloves, and 1 inch cinnamon—all ground together for this dish.

Red Tomatoes pureed-2

Cumin seeds (*Jeera*)-1/2 teaspoon

Clarified butter (*Ghee*)-4 tablespoon

Salt- 1 level teaspoon or to taste

Sugar-1/4 teaspoon

Water-4 cups

Method

Wash the rice well (in a vessel 3-4 times, but don't rub it lest the grains break) and let it naturally "dry", on an inclined plate, for 15-20 minutes. This helps enhance the aroma.

Roast the cottage cheese (*paneer*) or tofu on a dry pan and then cut into bite size pieces.

If using a pressure cooker:

In a pressure cooker, add the clarified butter and place it on your heat source.

When the butter warms up, add the cumin seeds. As soon as it starts giving a nice aroma, in less than a minute, add the onion slices and fry till translucent. Do please make sure that the spices brown and not burn, otherwise your dish will be totally spoiled.

Add the ginger and garlic. Stir for a minute.

Add all the vegetables except the *paneer* (cottage cheese) and stir well.

Now add the turmeric, chilli powder, coriander and *garam masala* and again stir well.

Pour the tomato puree over this mixture and stir till the tomatoes give off a nice aroma. That's the indication that they are getting cooked.

Add now the *paneer* (or tofu) and the blanched almonds.

Add the salt and sugar. Now add the rice.

Stir well.

Add the water.

Close the lid of the pressure cooker BUT remove the weight.

When steam starts escaping from the vent (don't worry, you will hear that typical sound), reduce the heat to minimum. In other words, if cooking on gas, turn the knob to SIM (mer).

Wait for 10 minutes and switch off the gas.

Take out the rice.

That's all. Your Vegetable *biryani* is ready.

This is a complete meal in itself.

If using a thick bottomed pan/vessel:

In a pan/vessel, add the clarified butter and place on fire.

When the butter warms up, add the cumin seeds. As soon as it starts giving a nice aroma, in less than a minute, add the onion slices and fry till translucent. Do please make sure that the spices brown and not burn, otherwise your dish will be totally spoiled.

Add the ginger and garlic. Stir for a minute.

Add all the vegetables except the *paneer* (cottage cheese) and stir well.

Now add the turmeric, chilli powder, coriander and *garam masala* and again stir well.

Pour the tomato puree over this mixture and stir till the tomatoes give off a nice aroma. That's the indication that they are getting cooked.

Add now the *paneer* (or *tofu*) and the blanched almonds.

Add the salt and sugar. Now add the rice.

Stir well.

Add the water.

Cover the pan/vessel with a well-fitting lid.

Reduce the heat to minimum. In other words, if cooking on gas, turn the knob to SIM (mer).

Let the rice cook for 20-25 minutes. Please check that the rice has cooked well.

Switch off the heat source and let the rice remain in the vessel for another 5 minutes.

Take out the rice.

That's all. Your Vegetable *biryani* is ready.

If using a rice cooker

In a pan/vessel, add the clarified butter and place on fire.

When the butter warms up, add the cumin seeds. As soon as it starts giving a nice aroma, in less than a minute, add the onion slices and fry till translucent. Do please make sure that the spices brown and not burn, otherwise your dish will be totally spoiled.

Add the ginger and garlic. Stir for a minute.

Add all the vegetables except the *paneer* (cottage cheese) and stir well.

Now add the turmeric, chilli powder, coriander and *garam masala* and again stir well.

Pour the tomato puree over this mixture and stir till the tomatoes give off a nice aroma. That's the indication that they are getting cooked.

Add now the *paneer* (or tofu) and the blanched almonds.

Add the salt and sugar. Now add the rice.

Stir well.

Switch off the heat source and put all the ingredients into the rice cooker.

Add the water.

Switch on the rice cooker and the let the rice cook. The rice cooker will switch off on its own when the rice is cooked.

Prep time: 20 minutes

Cooking time: 12 minutes with a pressure cooker; 20-25 minutes with a deep thick bottomed pan; and as indicated in the rice cooker manual

Total time: 32 minutes with a pressure cooker; 40-45 minutes with a deep thick bottomed pan

Navratna Pulao (Nine Jewels Rice Dish)

This is the ultimate vegetarian pilaf dish. Savour this on those really special occasions.

Ingredients

Long grain rice (Basmati)-2 cups

Cottage Cheese (*Paneer*) or *Tofu*-200 grams (7oz) (1 cup)

Peas-1/4 cup

Carrots cut into small pieces-1/4 cup

Cauliflower florets-1/4 cup

Raisins-2 tablespoon

Roasted Cashew nuts-3 tablespoon

(The method to roast the cashew nuts: in a small pan, add about a tablespoon of cooking oil. Put the pan on your heat source. When the oil heats up, add the cashew nuts and stir till they turn golden. Immediately remove the cashew nuts to a plate. Remember if you leave the cashew nuts in the pan, the hot oil will keep roasting the cashew nuts and burn them.)

Sliced Onion-1 (Medium)

Chopped Ginger-1 inch piece

Black Cumin seeds (*Shahi Jeera*)-1/2 teaspoon

Green Cardamom (*Chhoti elaichi*)-2

Brown Cardamom (*Badi elaichi*)-1

Cinnamon (*Dalchini*)-1/2 inch

Cloves (*Laung*)-4

Star aniseed-1

Mace (*Javitri*)-One small piece

Bay leaf (*Tejpatta*)-1

Clarified butter (*Ghee*)-4 tablespoon

Salt- 1 level teaspoon or to taste

Sugar-1/2 teaspoon

Few strands of saffron dissolved in ¼ cup milk

Water-4 cups

Method

Wash the rice well (in a vessel 3-4 times, but don't rub it lest the grains break) and let it naturally "dry", on an inclined plate, for 15-20 minutes. This helps enhance the aroma.

Roast the cottage cheese (*paneer*) or *tofu* on a dry pan and then cut into bite size pieces.

In a pan, add 2 tablespoon of clarified butter and gently roast peas, carrots and cauliflower one by one and keep aside.

If using a pressure cooker:

In a pressure cooker, add the clarified butter and place it on your heat source.

When the butter warms up, add the black cumin seeds along with the green cardamom, brown cardamom, cinnamon, cloves, star aniseed, mace and bay leaf.

As soon as these all start giving a nice aroma, in less than a minute, add the onion slices and fry till translucent. Do please make sure that the spices brown and not burn, otherwise your dish will be totally spoiled.

Add the ginger and stir for a minute.

Now add the rice along with the salt and sugar.

Stir well.

Add the roasted vegetables along with the *paneer* (cottage cheese) or tofu and again stir well.

Add the water, raisins and the saffron dissolved in milk.

Close the lid of the pressure cooker BUT remove the weight.

When steam starts escaping from the vent (don't worry, you will hear that typical sound), reduce the heat to minimum. In other words, if cooking on gas, turn the knob to SIM (mer).

Wait for 10 minutes and switch off the gas.

Take out the rice.

That's all. Your *Navratna pulao* is ready.

Before serving, sprinkle some roasted cashew nuts on the pulao and enjoy.

If using a thick bottomed pan/vessel:

In a pan/vessel, add the clarified butter and place on fire.

When the butter warms up, add the black cumin seeds along with the green cardamom, brown cardamom, cinnamon, cloves, star aniseed, mace and bay leaf.

As soon as these all start giving a nice aroma, in less than a minute, add the onion slices and fry till translucent.

Do please make sure that the spices brown and not burn, otherwise your dish will be totally spoiled.

Add the ginger and stir for a minute.

Now add the rice along with the salt and sugar.

Stir well.

Add the roasted vegetables along with the *paneer* (cottage cheese) or tofu and again stir well.

Add the water, raisins and the saffron dissolved in milk.

Cover the pan/vessel with a well-fitting lid.

Reduce the heat to minimum. In other words, if cooking on gas, turn the knob to SIM (mer).

Let the rice cook for 20-25 minutes. Please check that the rice has cooked well.

Switch off the heat source and let the rice remain in the vessel for another 5 minutes.

Take out the rice.

That's all. Your *Navratna pulao* is ready.

Before serving, sprinkle some roasted cashew nuts on the pulao and enjoy.

If using a rice cooker

In a pan/vessel, add the clarified butter and place on fire.

When the butter warms up, add the black cumin seeds along with the green cardamom, brown cardamom, cinnamon, cloves, star aniseed, mace and bay leaf.

As soon as these all start giving a nice aroma, in less than a minute, add the onion slices and fry till translucent.

Do please make sure that the spices brown and not burn, otherwise your dish will be totally spoiled.

Add the ginger and stir for a minute.

Now add the rice along with the salt and sugar.

Stir well.

Add the roasted vegetables along with the *paneer* (cottage cheese) or *tofu* and again stir well.

Add the water, raisins and the saffron dissolved in milk.

Switch off the heat source and put all the ingredients into the rice cooker.

Switch on the rice cooker and then let the rice cook. The rice cooker will switch off on its own when the rice is cooked.

Take out the rice.

That's all. Your *Navratna pulao* is ready.

Before serving, sprinkle some roasted cashew nuts on the *pulao* and enjoy.

Prep time: 20 minutes

Cooking time: 12 minutes with a pressure cooker; 20-25 minutes with a deep thick bottomed pan; and as indicated in the rice cooker manual

Total time: 32 minutes with a pressure cooker; 40-45 minutes with a deep thick bottomed pan

Stir Fried Rice

Try this dish when you have some left-over boiled rice lying around, and you will be pleasantly surprised at the transformation.

Ingredients

Cooked Boiled rice-1 cup

Cauliflower-a few florets

Broccoli-1 small

Carrot-1

French beans-a few

Peas- ¼ cup

Button Mushrooms-4

Chopped Onions-2

Chopped Garlic-4 cloves

Chopped Ginger-1 inch

Red chilli powder (only for flavour and not to make it hot)-1/4 teaspoon (you can add more if you like it hot)

Garam Masala (mixture of common Indian spices) - 1/4 teaspoon

Tip: If you can't get ready-made *garam masala* mixture from a nearby Indian store, you can make yours by using 1 black cardamom, 3 green cardamoms, 4 cloves, and 1 inch cinnamon–all ground together for this dish.

Turmeric (*Haldi*)-1/4 teaspoon

Salt- ½ teaspoon or to taste

Cooking Oil- 1 tablespoon

Method

Wash the vegetables and chop into small pieces.

In a wok, add the cooking oil and as soon as it warms up, add the chopped onions, garlic cloves and ginger.

As soon as the mixture starts giving off a nice aroma, add the vegetables.

Stir well.

Cover the wok, reduce the flame and let the vegetables steam in their own juice till cooked.

You may add the salt at this juncture along with turmeric, red chilli powder and *garam masala*.

Stir well.

Add the boiled rice, and again stir well so that all the ingredients are well mixed.

Switch off the heat source.

That's all. Your Stir Fried Rice is ready.

Prep time: 10 minutes

Cooking time: 20 minutes

Total time: 30 minutes

Stuffed *Parathas*

Yet another really delicious version of the Indian unleavened bread, *paratha*s are very popular for breakfasts, picnics and tours. Because these too are fried, somewhat more lightly than *pooris*, they do have a longer shelf life than *chapatis*.

Compared to *pooris*, *parathas* are much more amenable to all kinds of fillings. You also require much less cooking oil/*ghee* to cook *parathas*, which makes these the favourite of all economically conscious households as well as restaurants.

Here's then the recipes for five popular (stuffed with veggies) *parathas*.

Palak Paratha (Spinach *Paratha*)

Ingredients

Whole Wheat Flour-3 cups (enough for 5 *parathas*)

Salt-1 teaspoon (or to taste)

Cooking Oil-1 tablespoonful

Spinach – 250 grams (1 cup) (washed and chopped)

Water- 1 cup

Cooking Oil or Clarified Butter (*Ghee*) for roasting the *parathas*; *ghee* is preferred if you want the authentic taste.

Method

Place a vessel on your heat source.

Add a cup of water.

As soon as the water comes to a boil, add the spinach and boil for two minutes.

Switch off the heat source.

In a blender, put the boiled spinach along with the water and make a puree.

In a mixing bowl, mix together the wheat flour, salt and one tablespoon cooking oil.

Now make a firm dough by adding the spinach puree.

Cover the dough and leave for ½ an hour.

Take a large walnut sized dough and roll into a ball.

Spread 2 tablespoon of dry flour on a plate and roll this ball gently in it so that it is well covered with the dry flour. This helps in rolling out the dough as otherwise it will stick to the rolling board.

Now, flatten it on the rolling board as you do for *chapatis.*

When the dough is thin and round, spread a few drops of cooking oil on the surface and fold it in half. Spread a few more drops of cooking oil on this half and again fold to make a triangle.

Now, on the rolling board (*chakla*) and with a rolling pin *(belan)*, gently stretch this triangle to the biggest triangle you can manage or to the original size of the round *chapati*.

Put a griddle (*tawa*) on your heat source.

As soon as the griddle becomes hot, place the *paratha* on it.

Reduce the flame to medium and let the *paratha* cook on one side.

Flip over and let it cook on the other side.

Take a teaspoon of oil/*ghee* and spread it on the side facing you.

Flip over and repeat the process till the *paratha* gets a nice, crisp texture.

Line a casserole with a paper napkin and place the *paratha* inside it to keep it hot.

Repeat the process till all the *parathas* are made.

Enjoy your hot *parathas* with any vegetables or meat dish.

Prep time: 35 minutes

Cooking time: 5 minutes for 5 *parathas* @1 minute per *parathas*

Total time: 40 minutes

Methi Paratha (Fenugreek *Paratha*)

Ingredients

Whole Wheat Flour-3 cups (enough for 5 *parathas*)

Salt-1 teaspoon (or to taste)

Cooking Oil-1 tablespoonful

Fresh Fenugreek Leaves (*methi*) – 250 grams (1 cup) (chopped)

Kastoori Methi (dry) - 5 teaspoon

Water- 2 cup

Cooking Oil or Clarified Butter (*ghee*) for roasting the *parathas*; *ghee* is preferred if you want the authentic taste.

Method

Place a vessel on your heat source.

Add a cup of water.

As soon as the water comes to a boil, add the fenugreek leaves and boil for two minutes.

Switch off the heat source.

In a blender, put the boiled fenugreek leaves (without the water, as this water may be bitter) and make a puree.

In a mixing bowl, mix together the wheat flour, salt and one tablespoon cooking oil.

Now make a firm dough by adding the fenugreek puree and a cup of water.

Cover the dough and leave for ½ an hour.

Take a large walnut sized dough and roll into a ball.

Spread 2 tablespoon of dry flour on a plate and roll this ball gently in it so that it is well covered with the dry flour. This helps in rolling out the dough as otherwise it will stick to the rolling board.

Now, flatten it on the rolling board as you do for *chapatis.*

When the dough is thin and round, spread a few drops of cooking oil on the surface and fold it in half. Spread a few more drops of cooking oil on this half and again fold to make a triangle.

Now, on the rolling board (*chakla*) and with a rolling pin (*belan*), gently stretch this triangle to the biggest triangle you can manage or to the original size of the round *chapati.*

Put a griddle (*tawa*) on your heat source.

As soon as the griddle becomes hot, place the *paratha* on it.

Reduce the flame to medium and let the *paratha* cook on one side.

Flip over and let it cook on the other side.

Take a teaspoon of oil/*ghee* and spread it on the side facing you.

Sprinkle 1 teaspoon of crushed *kastoori methi* (on every *paratha*).

Flip over and repeat the process till the *paratha* gets a nice, crisp texture.

Line a casserole with a paper napkin and place the *paratha* inside it to keep it hot.

Repeat the process till all the *parathas* are made.

Enjoy your hot *parathas* with any vegetables or meat dish.

Prep time: 35 minutes

Cooking time: 5 minutes for 5 *parathas* @1 minute per *parathas*

Total time: 40 minutes

Mattar Bhara Paratha (Parathas Stuffed with Green Peas)

Ingredients

For Paratha

Whole Wheat Flour-3 cups (enough for 5 *parathas*)

Salt-1/2 teaspoon or to taste

Cooking Oil-1 tablespoonful

Luke Warm Water-1 cup

Cooking Oil or Clarified Butter (*ghee*) for roasting the *parathas*; *ghee* is preferred if you want the authentic taste.

For the filling:

Fresh green peas-1/2 cup

Cooking Oil-1 teaspoon

Cumin (*Jeera*) seeds-1/2 teaspoon

Finely Chopped Ginger-1/2 teaspoon

Garam Masala powder-1/4 teaspoon

Tip: If you can't get ready-made *garam masala* mixture from a nearby Indian store, you can make yours by using 1 black cardamom, 3 green cardamoms, 4 cloves, and 1 inch cinnamon—all ground together for this dish.

Red chilli powder (only for flavour and not to make it hot)-1/4 teaspoon (you can add more if you like it hot)

Salt: A pinch or to taste

Method

In a mixing bowl, mix together the wheat flour, salt and one tablespoon cooking oil.

Now make a firm dough by adding the water.

Cover the dough and leave for ½ an hour.

Meanwhile, in a wok, add the cooking oil (or *ghee*) and put it on your heat source.

As soon as the oil becomes warm, add the cumin seeds.

In a few seconds, when the cumin seeds become brown (please ensure that they don't burn), add the chopped ginger.

Now, add the green peas. Please don't add any water as the filling has to be dry.

Turn the heat/flame to low and add the salt, *garam masala* and red chilli powder.

Cover and cook for about 3 minutes till the peas are lightly cooked but not over cooked.

If you over cook, the peas will become mushy and will not be suitable for filling.

Turn off the heat source and in a blender, crush the peas to a paste.

Now, take a large walnut sized dough and roll into a ball.

Flatten this ball into a patty.

In the centre of this patty, place a tablespoon of the pea mixture.

Close the patty from all sides so that the mixture goes in the middle and is covered with a dough on all sides.

Again, flatten the dough gently with your hands giving it a round shape.

Spread 2 tablespoon of dry flour on a plate and roll this stuffed flattened dough gently in it so that it is well covered with the dry flour. This helps in rolling out the dough as otherwise it will stick to the rolling board.

Place the dough on a rolling board and flatten with a rolling pin till it gets a nice round shape.

Please press evenly while rolling out so that the pea mixture remains covered with dough.

Put a griddle on your heat source.

As soon as the griddle becomes hot, place the *paratha* on it.

Reduce the flame to medium and let the paratha cook on one side.

Flip over and let it cook on the other side.

Take a teaspoon of oil/*ghee* and spread it on the side facing you.

Flip over and repeat the process till the *Paratha* gets a nice, crisp texture.

Line a casserole with a paper napkin and place the *paratha* inside it to keep it hot.

Repeat the process till all the *parathas* are made.

Prep time: 35 minutes

Cooking time: 5 minutes for 5 *parathas* @1 minute per *parathas*

Total time: 40 minutes

***Gobi Bhara Paratha* (*Parathas* Stuffed with Cauliflower)**

Ingredients

For Paratha

Whole Wheat Flour-3 cups (enough for 5 *parathas*)

Salt-1/2 teaspoon or to taste

Cooking Oil-1 tablespoonful

Luke Warm Water-1 cup

Cooking Oil or Clarified Butter (*ghee*) for roasting the *parathas*; *ghee* is preferred if you want the authentic taste.

For the filling:

Cauliflower florets -1 cup (chopped fine)

Cooking Oil-1 teaspoon

Cumin (*Jeera*) seeds-1/2 teaspoon

Finely Chopped Ginger-1/2 teaspoon

Garam Masala powder-1/4 teaspoon

Tip: If you can't get ready-made *garam masala* mixture from a nearby Indian store, you can make yours by using 1 black cardamom, 3 green cardamoms, 4 cloves, and 1 inch cinnamon—all ground together for this dish.

Red chilli powder (only for flavour and not to make it hot)-1/4 teaspoon (you can add more if you like it hot)

Salt- to taste or ½ teaspoon

Method

In a mixing bowl, mix together the wheat flour, salt and one tablespoon cooking oil.

Now make a firm dough by adding the water.

Cover the dough and leave for ½ an hour.

Meanwhile, in a wok, add the cooking oil (or *ghee*) and put it on your heat source.

As soon as the oil becomes warm, add the cumin seeds.

In a few seconds, when the cumin seeds become brown (please ensure that they don't burn), add the chopped ginger.

Now, add the chopped cauliflower. Please don't add any water as the filling has to be dry.

Turn the heat/flame to low and add the salt, *garam masala* and red chilli powder.

Cover and cook for about 5 minutes till the cauliflower is lightly cooked but not over cooked.

Turn off the heat source. Remove the lid and let the cauliflower cool down.

Now, take a large walnut sized dough and roll into a ball.

Flatten this ball into a patty.

In the centre of this patty, place a tablespoon of the cauliflower mixture.

Close the patty from all sides so that the mixture goes in the middle and is covered with the dough on all sides.

Again, flatten the dough gently with your hands giving it a round shape.

Spread 2 tablespoon of dry flour on a plate and roll this stuffed flattened dough gently in it so that it is well covered with the dry flour. This helps in rolling out the dough as otherwise it will stick to the rolling board.

Now place the dough on a rolling board and flatten with a rolling pin till it gets a nice round shape.

Please press evenly while rolling out so that the cauliflower mixture remains covered with the dough.

Put a griddle (*tawa*) on your heat source.

As soon as the griddle becomes hot, place the *paratha* on it.

Reduce the flame to medium and let the *paratha* cook on one side.

Flip over and let it cook on the other side.

Take a teaspoon of oil/*ghee* and spread it on the side facing you.

Flip over and repeat the process till the *paratha* gets a nice, crisp texture.

Line a casserole with a paper napkin and place the *paratha* inside it to keep it hot.

Repeat the process till all the *parathas* are made.

Prep time: 35 minutes

Cooking time: 5 minutes for 5 *parathas* @1 minute per *parathas*

Total time: 40 minutes

Aloo Paratha (*Parathas* Stuffed with Potato)

Ingredients

For Paratha

Whole Wheat Flour-3 cups (enough for 5 *parathas*)

Salt-1/2 teaspoon or to taste

Cooking Oil-1 tablespoonful

Luke Warm Water-1 cup

Cooking Oil or Clarified Butter (*ghee*) for roasting the *parathas*; *ghee* is preferred if you want the authentic taste.

For the filling:

Potato-250 grams or 1 cup (boiled, peeled and finely mashed)

Cooking Oil-1 tablespoon

Cumin (*Jeera*) seeds-1/2 teaspoon

Finely Chopped Onion- 1

Garam Masala powder-1/4 teaspoon

Tip: If you can't get ready-made *garam masala* mixture from a nearby Indian store, you can make yours by using 1 black cardamom, 3 green cardamoms, 4 cloves, and 1 inch cinnamon—all ground together for this dish.

Red chilli powder (only for flavour and not to make it hot)-1/4 teaspoon (you can add more if you like it hot)

Dry Mango (*Amchur*) powder- 1 teaspoon

Fresh Coriander leaves- 2 tablespoon (chopped)

Green Chillies (deseeded and chopped) - 1

Salt- to taste or ½ teaspoon

Method

In a mixing bowl, mix together the wheat flour, salt and one tablespoon cooking oil.

Now make a firm dough by adding the water.

Cover the dough and leave for ½ an hour.

Meanwhile, in a wok, add the cooking oil (or *ghee*) and put it on your heat source.

As soon as the oil becomes warm, add the cumin seeds.

In a few seconds, when the cumin seeds become brown (please ensure that they don't burn), add the chopped onions.

Stir till the onions become translucent.

Turn the heat/flame to low and add the salt, *garam masala, amchur*, and red chilli powder. Stir.

Now add the mashed potato, green chillies and the chopped coriander leaves.

Mix well and turn off the heat source.

Let the potato mixture cool down.

Now, take a large walnut sized dough and roll into a ball.

Flatten this ball into a patty.

In the centre of this patty, place a tablespoon of the potato mixture.

Close the patty from all sides so that the mixture goes in the middle and is covered with a dough.

Again, flatten the dough gently with your hands giving it a round shape.

Spread 2 tablespoon of dry flour on a plate and roll this stuffed flattened dough gently in it so that it is well covered with the dry flour. This helps in rolling out the dough as otherwise it will stick to the rolling board.

Now place the dough on a rolling board and flatten with a rolling pin till it gets a nice round shape.

Please press evenly while rolling out so that the potato mixture remains covered with the dough on all sides.

Put a griddle (*tawa*) on your heat source.

As soon as the griddle becomes hot, place the *paratha* on it.

Reduce the flame to medium and let the *paratha* cook on one side.

Flip over and let it cook on the other side.

Take a teaspoon of oil/*ghee* and spread it on the side facing you.

Flip over and repeat the process till the *paratha* gets a nice, crisp texture.

Line a casserole with a paper napkin and place the *paratha* inside it to keep it hot.

Repeat the process till all the *parathas* are made.

Prep time: 35 minutes

Cooking time: 5 minutes for 5 *parathas* @1 minute per *parathas*

Total time: 40 minutes

Chapter 5: The Raj Effect

—Dione Lucas

These are dishes which have obviously been inspired by the way the British cooked their meals while ruling over India for almost 200 years. We present 15 such gems here.

The most common among these are the soups that the Brits couldn't do without and which the Indian cuisine doesn't patronize at all. We feature some six of them here.

Next are some baked dishes. We pick up just four here, in addition to a student dish.

Finally, we have the cutlets and chops. We present four of them in this chapter.

N.B. Those looking for an authentic Indian taste, however, may like to skip this chapter.

Making Pumpkin Soup

Serves 2

Ingredients

Ripe yellow pumpkin-250 grams or 9oz (1 cup) (all chopped up)

Onion-1 (chopped up)

Garlic-2 cloves

Cinnamon (*Dalchini*) powder-1 teaspoon

Milk-1/2 cup

Water-2 cups

Butter- 1 teaspoon

Salt- ½ teaspoon or to taste

Method

In a deep pan, put the butter and add the chopped onions and garlic.

Put it on fire and sauté till the onion is translucent.

Add the chopped up pumpkin and stir well.

Add 2 cups of water and bring the mixture to boil.

Reduce the heat to minimum (SIM if on gas) and cook till the pumpkins become soft.

Switch off the heat and let the mixture cool down.

Put this mixture in a blender and blend well.

Strain this all back into the pan.

Add the cinnamon powder, milk and salt and bring to a boil.

Switch off the heat and serve.

It is suggested that you taste the soup before serving so that you may adjust the salt according to your taste.

Your simple yet exotic pumpkin soup is ready.

Prep time: 10 minutes

Cooking time: 15 minutes

Total time: 25 minutes

Making Tomato Soup

Serves 2

Ingredients

Ripe Tomatoes-500 grams or 18oz (2 cups) (chopped up)

Onion-1 (chopped up)

Garlic-2 cloves (chopped up)

Ginger-1 inch piece (chopped up)

Milk-1/2 cup

Corn Flour-1 heap tablespoon

Salt, sugar and pepper- to taste

Water—2 cups

Method

Put all the chopped up ingredients (EXCEPT MILK, SALT, SUGAR AND CORN FLOUR) in a deep pan along with 2 cups of water.

Put the pan on fire.

After the mixture starts boiling, reduce the heat and cook till the tomatoes are well cooked (approximately 7 minutes).

Switch off the heat source and let the mixture cool down.

Take out the mixture and blend it well in a blender.

Strain this mixture back into the pan and bring it to a boil.

Add the corn flour, dissolved in half a cup of milk.

Add also the salt, pepper and sugar.

Let the mixture boil for 2 minutes.

Turn off the heat source.

Your lovely homemade tomato soup is ready.

It is suggested that you taste the soup before serving so that you adjust the salt and sugar according to your taste.

Prep time: 8 minutes

Cooking time: 10 minutes

Total time: 18 minutes

Cauliflower/Broccoli Soup

Serves 2

Ingredients

Cauliflower/Broccoli florets-250 grams (9oz) (1 cup)-all chopped

Onion-1 (chopped)

Garlic-2 cloves

Cinnamon (*Dalchini*) powder-1 teaspoon

Milk-1/2 cup

Water-2 cups

Butter- 1 teaspoon

Salt- ½ teaspoon or to taste

Note: You may add some cheese to your soup if you like it that way.

Method

In a deep pan, put the butter and add the chopped onions and garlic.

Put it on fire and sauté till the onions are translucent.

Add the chopped cauliflower/broccoli florets and stir well.

Add 2 cups of water and bring the mixture to boil.

Reduce the heat to minimum (SIM if on gas) and cook till the cauliflower/broccoli florets become soft.

Switch off the heat and let the mixture cool down.

Put this mixture in a blender and blend well.

Pour this all back into the pan.

Add the cinnamon powder, milk and salt and bring to a boil.

Switch off the heat and serve.

It is suggested that you taste the soup before serving so that you may adjust the salt according to your taste.

Your simple yet exotic cauliflower/broccoli soup is ready.

Prep time: 10 minutes

Cooking time: 15 minutes

Total time: 25 minutes

Mushroom Soup

Serves 2

Ingredients

Button Mushroom-250 grams (9oz) (1 cup)–all chopped

Onion-1 (chopped)

Garlic-2 cloves

Cinnamon (*Dalchini*) powder-1 teaspoon

Milk-1/2 cup

Water-1 cup

Butter- 1 teaspoon

Salt- ½ teaspoon to taste

Note: You may add thyme, rosemary and parsley too for added flavours.

Method

In a deep pan, put the butter and add the chopped onions and garlic.

Put it on fire and sauté till the onions are translucent.

Add the chopped mushrooms and stir well.

Add 1 cup of water and bring the mixture to boil.

Reduce the heat to minimum (SIM if on gas) and cook till the mushrooms become soft.

Switch off the heat and let the mixture cool down.

Put this mixture in a blender and blend well.

Pour this all back into the pan.

Add the cinnamon powder, milk and salt and bring to a boil.

Switch off the heat and serve.

It is suggested that you taste the soup before serving so that you may adjust the salt according to your taste.

Your mushroom soup is ready.

Prep time: 10 minutes

Cooking time: 15 minutes

Total time: 25 minutes

Cabbage Soup

Serves 2

Ingredients

Cabbage-300 grams (10oz) (1 cup)

Ripe Tomatoes-300 grams (10oz) (1 cup)

Red Bell Pepper-1

Carrots-2

Onion-1

Garlic-2 cloves

Ginger-1 inch piece

Salt, sugar and pepper- to taste

Water—1 cup

Method

Wash and chop all the vegetables.

Put all the chopped vegetables in a deep pan along with 1 cup of water.

Put the pan on fire.

After the mixture starts boiling, reduce the heat and cook till the vegetables are well cooked (approximately 7 minutes).

Switch off the heat source and let the mixture cool down.

Take out the mixture and blend it well in a blender.

Pour the mixture back into the pan.

Now, add the salt, pepper and sugar.

Let the mixture boil for 2 minutes.

Turn off the heat source.

Your lovely homemade cabbage soup is ready.

It is suggested that you taste the soup before serving so that you adjust the salt and sugar according to your taste. You can add more water if you find that the consistency of the soup is too thick.

Prep time: 8 minutes

Cooking time: 10 minutes

Total time: 18 minutes

Making Mixed Vegetable Soup

Serves 2

Ingredients

French beans-50 grams (2oz) (3 tablespoon)

Carrots-50 grams (2oz) (3 tablespoon)

Potatoes-1 (peeled)

Broccoli/Cauliflower-50 grams (2oz) (3 tablespoon)

Wheat flour-1 heaped tablespoon

Milk-1/2 cup

Butter-1 tablespoon

Salt and pepper to taste

Water-2-3 cups (depending upon how thick you like the soup. Less water will make the soup thicker and more will make the soup lighter)

Method

Chop finely all the vegetables.

In a deep pan, add the butter and put it on the fire.

As the butter melts, add all the vegetables and stir well.

When the vegetables start changing their colour, add the wheat flour and again stir well for 2 minutes.

Now, add the milk, water, the salt and pepper. Let the mixture boil.

Reduce the heat and cook till the vegetables are done.

That's all. Your healthy vegetable soup is ready in a jiffy.

Prep time: 5-10 minutes (depends if you need to cut vegetables)

Cooking time: 10 minutes

Total time: 15-20 minutes

Vegetables *au Gratin*

Ingredients

Cauliflower-a few florets

Broccoli-1 small

Carrot-1

French beans-a few

Peas shelled-1/4 cup

Snow peas- a few

Bell Pepper-1 (sliced)

Butter-2 tablespoon (1 tablespoon for sautéing vegetables and the other for making the white sauce)

Salt and Pepper to taste

Note: Feel free to add any other seasonings/herbs of your choice

Wheat flour–1 tablespoon

Milk-250 ml (1 cup; at room temperature)

Cheese Cheddar-25 grams (1oz) (1 tablespoon)–grated (for adding more protein to this dish)

Method

First sauté the mixed vegetables, which means:

Wash the vegetables thoroughly.

Wherever needed, cut in bite size pieces (except for the bell pepper, which is to be thinly sliced but NOT to be sautéed).

Switch on your heat source and put a pan on it.

Add the butter to the pan and let it melt.

Add all the vegetables and stir well.

Tip: Please don't add salt to the vegetables because the white sauce will contain sufficient amount of salt.

Reduce the heat to minimum (SIM on a gas stove), add the water and cover the pan.

You will see the steam escaping after a while.

Keep checking till the water has dried.

You may also use a fork to poke the vegetables to ensure that they have been cooked properly.

Your vegetables are now ready. You can decorate your vegetables au gratin with finely sliced bell peppers which impart a nice colour and flavour to this dish.

Next, Make the White Sauce, which means:

Switch on your heat source and put a pan on it.

Add a tablespoon of butter to the pan and let it melt.

As the butter melts, add the flour.

Gently mix/sauté the flour with the butter making sure that the flour DOES NOT turn brown.

Switch off the heat source and let the mixture cool down.

When the mixture comes to room temperature, gently add the milk (also at room temperature) and mix well to ensure that no lumps are formed.

Return this to the fire.

Add the cheese and a bit of salt.

As soon as the mixture thickens, your white sauce is ready.

Now add the vegetables to the white sauce and mix well.

Congratulations!! Your Vegetables *au gratin* is ready.

Preparation time: 10 minutes

Cooking time: 7 minutes

Total: 17 minutes

Aubergine *au Gratin*

Serves 2

Ingredients

Round purple aubergine (big) -1

Butter-2 tablespoon (1 tablespoon for roasting the aubergines and the other for making the white sauce)

Salt and Pepper to taste

Wheat flour–2 tablespoon

Milk-500 ml (2 cups; at room temperature)

Cheese Cheddar-50 grams (2oz) (2 tablespoon)—grated

Note: Feel free to add any other herbs/seasonings of your choice

Method

Wash the aubergine well and slice into round pieces with the skin.

Sprinkle a little salt on the aubergine slices.

In a non-stick pan, add 1 tablespoon butter and let it warm up.

Gently roast the aubergines on both sides till cooked.

Place the aubergines in a baking dish.

Now make the white sauce:

Switch on your heat source and put a pan on it.

Add a tablespoon of butter to the pan and let it melt.

As the butter melts, add the flour.

Gently mix/sauté the flour with the butter making sure that the flour DOES NOT turn brown.

Switch off the heat source and let the mixture cool down.

When the mixture comes to room temperature, gently add the milk (also at room temperature) and mix well to ensure that no lumps are formed.

Return this to the fire.

Add the cheese and a bit of salt.

As soon as the mixture thickens, your white sauce is ready.

Pour this sauce over the aubergines and bake for 5 minutes at 150 degrees C (300 degrees F) in a pre-heated oven.

In order to save time, I suggest that you start pre-heating the oven when you start roasting the aubergines.

Prep time: 5 minutes

Cooking time: 15 minutes

Total time: 20 minutes

Veggies in Pizza/Pasta Sauce

This is a quickie student dish. But it is full of so many veggies, that it can become a full meal.

Serves 2

Ingredients

Cauliflower-a few florets

Broccoli-1 small

Carrot-1

French beans-a few

Peas shelled-1/4 cup

Snow peas- a few

Chopped Onion-1

Garlic-4 cloves

Butter-1 tablespoon

Water-2 tablespoon

Salt and Pepper to taste

Pizza/pasta sauce-3 tablespoon

Method

Wash the vegetables thoroughly.

Wherever needed, cut in bite size pieces.

Switch on your heat source and put a pan on it.

Add the butter to the pan and let it melt.

Add the chopped onion and garlic and stir well till the onions become translucent.

Now, add all the vegetables and stir well.

When the vegetables start changing colour, add a pinch of salt and keep stirring.

Reduce the heat to minimum (SIM on a gas stove), add the water and cover the pan.

You will see that the steam starts escaping after a while.

Keep checking till the water has dried. Now add the Pizza/Pasta sauce and pepper.

Stir well.

That's all. Your vegetables are ready.

Tip: You may also use a fork to poke the vegetables once in a while to ensure that they have been cooked properly.

Preparation time: 5 minutes

Cooking time: 7 minutes

Total: 12 minutes

Potato Waffles

Serves 2

Ingredients

Potatoes-4

Milk-250 ml (1 cup)

Whole Wheat Flour-2 tablespoon

Low Fat Fresh Cream-1 tablespoonful

Egg-1

Cooking Oil-1 tablespoon

Salt and Pepper to taste

Chopped Fresh Coriander/Parsley leaves-1 tablespoon

Method

Boil the potatoes till cooked (roughly 10 minutes).

Peel and mash the potatoes.

Beat the egg well and mix with flour and cream.

Mix this mixture with the mashed potatoes.

Gradually add the milk, salt and pepper and the fresh coriander/parsley.

Mix well.

The batter will be fairly liquid.

Pre-heat the waffle maker and brush both plates with a little oil.

Pour the mixture into the lower plates.

Close the waffle tray and cook for about 5 minutes or till the waffle gets a nice golden colour.

Gently lift from the waffle tray and enjoy!

Prep time: 5 minutes

Cooking time: 10 minutes for boiling potatoes + 5 minutes in the waffle maker

Total time: 20 minutes

Baked Mushrooms Stuffed with Cheese

Serves 2

Ingredients

Button mushrooms-200 grams (7oz) (1 cup)

Paneer (Indian Cottage Cheese)/*Tofu*-2 tablespoon

Grated Cheddar Cheese—2 tablespoon

Fresh herbs to your taste-1 teaspoon

Pepper-1/4 teaspoon

Sugar-1/4 teaspoon

Salt- ½ teaspoon or to taste

Whole Wheat Flour-1 heaped tablespoon

Method

Remove the stalk (the bottom portion) from the button mushrooms so that each mushroom becomes like a little hollowed bowl.

Next, in a bowl, mix together all the ingredients except the flour.

Make small balls of this mixture and place a ball inside each hollowed button mushroom.

Now dip the filled side into the flour and place in a baking tray (flour side up) so that the fillings don't leak out.

Place all the mushrooms in this manner.

Place the baking tray in the oven at 150 degrees Centigrade (300 degrees Fahrenheit) and bake for about 15 minutes or till the mushrooms are well cooked.

That's all. Your stuffed mushrooms are now ready to be served.

Prep time: 10 minutes

Cooking time: 15 minutes

Total time: 25 minutes

Stuffed Capsicum in a Tomato Base

Serves 2

Ingredients

Capsicum-4

Mashed Boiled Potatoes-2

Chopped Onion-1

Chopped Garlic-2 cloves

Cinnamon powder-a pinch

Sugar-1/2 teaspoon

Salt- ½ teaspoon or to taste

For the gravy:

Tomato puree-250 ml (1 cup)

Black Pepper-1/4 teaspoon

Sugar-1/2 teaspoon

Salt- ½ teaspoon or to taste

Fresh Low Fat Cream-100 ml (1/2 cup)

Cooking Oil-1 tablespoon

Method

Cut the capsicum in half and remove all the seeds.

In a bowl, mix together all the ingredients (except the ones for the gravy).

In each capsicum, stuff a tablespoon of this mixture.

In a wok, place the cooking oil and put it on your heat source.

Add the tomato puree, the sugar, salt and black pepper and stir well for a few minutes.

Add the cream and switch off the heat source.

In a baking dish, pour the tomato puree mixture first.

Next place each capsicum separately in this mixture, with the filling portion facing up.

Bake in the oven at 150 degrees C (300 degrees F) for about 10 minutes.

That's all. Your stuffed capsicum is ready.

Prep time: 10 minutes

Cooking time: 10 minutes for boiling potatoes + 10 minutes

Total time: 30 minutes

Marshall Cutlets

Serves 3-4

Ingredients

Potatoes (boiled, peeled and mashed)-1/2 Kg (18oz) (2 cups)

French Beans- 250 grams- 1 cup (chopped fine)

Carrots- 250 grams- 1 cup (chopped fine)

Ginger paste- 1 teaspoon

Garlic paste- 1 teaspoon

Green Chillies (deseeded and finely chopped) - 2

Black pepper (crushed) - ¼ teaspoon

Garam Masala- ½ teaspoon

Tip: If you can't get ready-made *garam masala* mixture from a nearby Indian store, you can make yours by using 1 black cardamom, 3 green cardamoms, 4 cloves, and 1 inch cinnamon—all ground together for this dish.

Tomato ketchup- 2 tablespoon

Lemon juice- 1 teaspoon

Peanuts- ½ cup (fried or baked)

Fresh coriander (Cilantro) leaves (finely chopped) - 2 tablespoon

Bread slices- 2

Bread crumbs- ½ cup

Salt- ½ teaspoon or to taste

Flour (any that you prefer) - 2 tablespoon dissolve in ½ cup water for coating the cutlets

Cooking Oil (enough to deep fry) - depends on the size of your wok/deep frying pan. If using an air fryer, two tablespoon may be enough.

Method using a wok/pan

Boil and peel the potatoes and then mash it with a fork.

In a wok, put 1 tablespoon cooking oil and put it on your heat source.

As soon as the oil warms up, add the garlic-ginger paste and sauté for 2 minutes.

Now add the beans and carrots and sauté for a few more minutes at reduced heat levels.

Meanwhile dip the bread pieces in water and immediately squeeze out all the water. Keep aside.

As soon as the beans and carrots are lightly cooked, add the green chillies, black pepper, *garam masala*, tomato ketchup, and lemon juice, and stir well.

Now, add the mashed potatoes and mix well.

Let the mixture dry somewhat which should hardly take a minute or two. Now, turn off the heat source and take out the veggie mixture in a serving bowl.

Add the soaked bread pieces, coriander leaves, and the peanuts and mix well.

Take a tablespoon of this mixture in your hands and squeeze it into an oblong shape.

Repeat till all the mixture is thus shaped.

Dip each cutlet in the dissolve flour and roll on the plate with the bread crumbs and keep aside.

Heat oil in a frying pan or wok.

Take 3-4 pieces of the cutlet, and gently slide into the hot oil.

Gently turn them around and take out from the oil when they are nice and golden brown.

Remove to a plate and add the next batch to the oil.

Repeat till all the cutlets are fried.

Please ensure that the cutlets does not burn.

That's all. Your Marshall Cutlets are ready.

If using an air fryer

Pre-heat the air fryer at 200 degree C (392 degrees F) for 5 minutes.

Follow all the preparatory steps listed above till you come to deep frying in oil.

Now, with a silicon brush, gently brush the coated cutlets with a little oil on all sides.

Place the cutlets in the air fryer in a way that all pieces remain separate and NOT on top of one another.

Air-fry for 8 minutes at 200 degree C (392 degrees F).

Repeat till all the cutlets are air-fried.

Prep time: 10 minutes; plus 5 minutes if using the air fryer

Cooking time: 10 minutes (if potatoes are already boiled) otherwise include the time for boiling the potatoes; plus 2 minutes @ each batch for wok/pan; 8 minutes@ each batch for air fryer

Total time: Approximately 35 minutes for wok/pan; 65 minutes for air fryer

---

***Paneer* Cutlets**

Serves 3-4

Ingredients

Paneer (cottage cheese)-1/2 Kg (18oz) (2 cups)

Green Peas- 250 grams- 1 cup

Carrots- 250 grams- 1 cup (chopped fine)

Ginger paste- 1 teaspoon

Garlic paste- 1 teaspoon

Green Chillies (deseeded and finely chopped) - 2

Black pepper (crushed) - ¼ teaspoon

Garam Masala- ½ teaspoon

Tip: If you can't get ready-made *garam masala* mixture from a nearby Indian store, you can make yours by using 1 black cardamom, 3 green cardamoms, 4 cloves, and 1 inch cinnamon—all ground together for this dish.

Tomato ketchup- 2 tablespoon

Peanuts- ½ cup (fried or baked)

Fresh coriander (Cilantro) leaves (finely chopped) - 2 tablespoon

Bread slices- 4

Bread crumbs- ½ cup

Salt- ½ teaspoon or to taste

Flour (any that you prefer) - 2 tablespoon dissolved in ½ cup water for coating the cutlets

Cooking Oil (enough to deep fry) - depends on the size of your wok/deep frying pan. If using an air fryer, two tablespoon may be enough.

Method using a wok/pan

Mash the *paneer* with a fork and keep aside.

In a wok, put 1 tablespoon cooking oil and put it on your heat source.

As soon as the oil warms up, add the garlic-ginger paste and sauté for 2 minutes.

Now add the peas and carrots and sauté for a few more minutes at reduced heat levels.

Meanwhile dip the bread pieces in water and immediately squeeze out all the water. Keep aside.

As soon as the peas and carrots are lightly cooked, add the green chillies, black pepper, *garam masala*, and tomato ketchup and stir well.

Now, add the mashed *paneer* and mix well.

Turn off the heat source and take out the mixture in a serving bowl.

Add the soaked bread pieces, coriander leaves, and the peanuts and mix well.

Take a tablespoon of this mixture in your hands and squeeze it into an oblong shape.

Repeat till all the mixture is thus shaped.

Dip each cutlet in the dissolved flour and roll on the plate with the bread crumbs and keep aside.

Heat oil in a frying pan or wok.

Take 3-4 pieces of the cutlet, and gently slide into the hot oil.

Gently turn them around and take out from the oil when they are nice and golden brown.

Remove to a plate and add the next batch to the oil.

Repeat till all the cutlets are fried.

Please ensure that the cutlets do not burn.

That's all. Your *Paneer* Cutlets are ready.

If using an air fryer

Pre-heat the air fryer at 200 degree C (392 degrees F) for 5 minutes.

Follow all the preparatory steps listed above till you come to deep frying in oil.

Now, with a silicon brush, gently brush the coated cutlets with a little oil on all sides.

Place the cutlets in the air fryer in a way that all pieces remain separate and NOT on top of one another.

Air-fry for 8 minutes at 200 degree C (392 degrees F).

Repeat till all the cutlets are air-fried.

Prep time: 10 minutes; plus 5 minutes if using the air fryer

Cooking time: 10 minutes; plus 2 minutes @ each batch for wok/pan; 8 minutes@ each batch for air fryer

Total time: Approximately 35 minutes for wok/pan; 65 minutes for air fryer

Veggie Chops

This dish uses *garam masala* and is more suited for dinners than snacks.

Serves 3-4

Ingredients

French Beans- 250 grams- 1 cup (chopped fine)

Carrots- 250 grams- 1 cup (chopped fine)

Cauliflower- 250 grams- 1 cup (chopped fine)

Onions (chopped) - 1

Ginger (chopped) - 1 teaspoon

Garlic (chopped) - 1 teaspoon

Green Chillies (deseeded and finely chopped) - 2

Black Pepper (crushed) - ¼ teaspoon

Cumin seeds (*Jeera*) - ½ teaspoon

Garam Masala- ½ teaspoon

Tip: If you can't get ready-made *garam masala* mixture from a nearby Indian store, you can make yours by using 1 black cardamom, 3 green cardamoms, 4 cloves, and 1 inch cinnamon—all ground together for this dish.

Tomato ketchup- 1 tablespoon

Fresh Coriander (Cilantro) leaves (finely chopped) - 2 tablespoon

Raisins- 1 tablespoon

Salt- 1/4 teaspoon or to taste

Cooking oil- 1 tablespoon

For the covering:

Potatoes (boiled and mashed) - 1/2 Kg (18oz) (2 cups)

Salt and pepper to taste

Flour (any that you prefer) - 2 tablespoon

Bread crumbs- ½ cup

Water- 1/4 cup

AND

Cooking Oil (enough to deep fry) - depends on the size of your wok/deep frying pan. If using an air fryer, two tablespoon may be enough.

Method using a wok/pan

Place a pan on your heat source and put one tablespoon of cooking oil.

As soon as the oil heats up, add the cumin seeds.

In a few seconds the cumin will splutter and brown. Immediately add the chopped onion, garlic and ginger.

Sauté till these start changing colour and giving off a nice aroma.

Now add the vegetables and sauté for a few more minutes at reduced heat levels.

Now add rest of the ingredients (except the ones kept for the covering). Mix well.

Switch off the heat source.

Meanwhile take the mashed potatoes and add salt and pepper.

Take two tablespoon of this potato mixture in your hands and make a hole in the middle.

Fill the hole up with the veggie mixture and roll into an egg shape.

Make sure that the veggie mixture is covered well with the potato on all sides.

Repeat till all the chops are thus shaped.

Now make the coating:

In another bowl, mix together the flour and the water.

In a plate, spread the bread crumb.

Take out one piece of the chop at a time, and dip it into the flour mixture.

Then take the chop out and gently roll it on the plate with breadcrumbs so that it is evenly coated.

Do this with all the veggie chops.

Heat oil in a frying pan or wok.

Take 2 veggie chops and gently slide into the hot oil.

Gently turn them around and take out from the oil when they are nice and golden brown.

Remove to a plate and add the next batch to the oil.

Repeat till all the chops are fried.

Please ensure that the chops do not burn.

That's all. Your Veggie Chops are ready.

If using an air fryer

Pre-heat the air fryer at 200 degree C (392 degrees F) for 5 minutes. Follow all the preparatory steps listed above till you come to deep frying in oil. Now, with a silicon brush, gently brush the coated veggie chops with a little oil on all sides.

Place the chops in the air fryer in a way that all pieces remain separate and NOT on top of one another.

Air-fry for 8 minutes at 200 degree C (392 degrees F).

Repeat till all the chops are air-fried.

Prep time: 20 minutes; plus 5 minutes if using the air fryer

Cooking time: 2 minutes @ each batch for wok/pan; 8 minutes@ each batch for air fryer

Total time: Approximately 40 minutes for wok/pan; 65 minutes for air fryer

Paneer **Chops**

This dish too uses *garam masala* and is more suited for dinners than snacks.

Serves 3-4

Ingredients

Paneer- 250 grams (9oz) (1 cup)

Cheddar Cheese- 100 grams (half cup)

Onions (chopped) - 1

Ginger (chopped) - 1 teaspoon

Garlic (chopped) - 1 teaspoon

Green Chillies (deseeded and finely chopped) - 2

Black Pepper (crushed) - ¼ teaspoon

Cumin seeds (*Jeera*) - ½ teaspoon

Garam Masala- ½ teaspoon

Tip: If you can't get ready-made *garam masala* mixture from a nearby Indian store, you can make yours by using 1 black cardamom, 3 green cardamoms, 4 cloves, and 1 inch cinnamon—all ground together for this dish.

Tomato ketchup- 1 tablespoon

Fresh Coriander (Cilantro) leaves (finely chopped) - 2 tablespoon

Raisins- 1 tablespoon

Salt- 1/4 teaspoon or to taste

Cooking oil- 1 tablespoon

For the covering:

Potatoes (boiled and mashed) - 1/2 Kg (18oz) (2 cups)

Salt and pepper to taste

Flour (any that you prefer) - 2 tablespoon

Bread crumbs- ½ cup

Water- 1/4 cup

AND

Cooking Oil (enough to deep fry) - depends on the size of your wok/deep frying pan. If using an air fryer, two tablespoon may be enough.

Method using the wok/pan

Mash the *paneer* with a fork and keep aside.

Place a pan on your heat source and put one tablespoon of cooking oil.

As soon as the oil heats up, add the cumin seeds.

In a few seconds the cumin will splutter and brown. Immediately add the chopped onion, garlic and ginger.

Sauté till these start changing colour and giving off a nice aroma.

Now add the *paneer* and rest of the ingredients (except the ones kept for the covering). Mix well.

Switch off the heat source.

Meanwhile take the mashed potatoes and add salt and pepper.

Take two tablespoon of this potato mixture in your hands and make a hole in the middle.

Fill the hole up with the *paneer* mixture and roll into an egg shape.

Make sure that the *paneer* mixture is covered well with the potato on all sides.

Repeat till all the chops are thus shaped.

Now make the coating:

In another bowl, mix together the flour and the water.

In a plate, spread the bread crumb.

Take out one piece of the chop at a time, and dip it into the flour mixture.

Then take the chop out and gently roll it on the plate with breadcrumbs so that it is evenly coated.

Do this with all the *paneer* chops.

Heat oil in a frying pan or wok.

Take 2 *paneer* chops and gently slide into the hot oil.

Gently turn them around and take out from the oil when they are nice and golden brown.

Remove to a plate and add the next batch to the oil.

Repeat till all the chops are fried.

Please ensure that the chops do not burn.

That's all. Your *Paneer* Chops are ready.

If using an air fryer

Pre-heat the air fryer at 200 degree C (392 degrees F) for 5 minutes. Follow all the preparatory steps listed above till you come to deep frying in oil. Now, with a silicon brush, gently brush the coated *paneer* chops with a little oil on all sides.

Place the chops in the air fryer in a way that all pieces remain separate and NOT on top of one another.

Air-fry for 8 minutes at 200 degree C (392 degrees F).

Repeat till all the chops are air-fried.

Prep time: 20 minutes; plus 5 minutes if using the air fryer

Cooking time: 2 minutes @ each batch for wok/pan; 8 minutes@ each batch for air fryer

Total time: Approximately 40 minutes for wok/pan; 65 minutes for air fryer

Chapter 6: Making Desserts with Veggies-The Indian Way

–Doug Larson

No Doug, we beg to differ. You need to come to India to see how we turn ordinary veggies in to not only great curries but delicious desserts.

And, without adding any bacon, of course!

Just savour a sample of the eight great Veggie Puddings that we shall now present.

And we guarantee you will soon be asking for more.

Gajar Ka Halwa **(Carrot *Halwa*)**

This is the classic winter dessert that you will find being served in most weddings in North India. We present, however, a short-cut and lower calorie version here.

Serves 3-4

Ingredients

Full cream milk-2 litre (4 US pints liquid) (8 cups)

Carrot-2 cup- 500 grams (grated)

Sugar to taste - (start with 6 tablespoons)

Milk Powder-6 tablespoons

Green Cardamom (*Chhoti Elaichi*)-3 crushed

Raisins- 50 grams (3 tablespoon)

Walnuts- 50 grams (3 tablespoon) (chopped)

Cashew Nuts- 50 grams (3 tablespoon) (chopped)

Ghee (clarified butter) - 2 table spoons

Method

In a heavy bottomed wok, bring the milk to boil.

Add the grated carrots.

Keep stirring on low heat making sure that NOTHING BURNS.

As the mixture begins to thicken, add the milk powder, and the cardamom.

Stir well and keep stirring till the mixture becomes almost dry.

Now add the sugar, raisins, walnuts and cashew nuts.

Keep stirring till all the sugar is melted and well blended.

Keep stirring till the mixture again becomes dry.

Now add the *ghee* and stir for five more minutes.

Switch off the heat source.

That's all. Your delicious *Gajar ka Halwa* (Carrot *Halwa*) is ready.

You can either have it hot as some like it. Or you could let it cool down and then put it in the fridge and have it when it is cold.

Prep time: 10 minute

Cooking time: 60 minutes

Total time: 70 minutes

Gobi Ka Kheer (Cauliflower Pudding)

This is a take on that North Indian dessert kheer that the gods are very fond of. So don't be surprised to be served this kheer when it is cauliflower season.

Serves 3-4

Ingredients

Full cream milk-1 litre (2 US pints liquid) (4 cups)

Cauliflower-1 cup- 250 grams (washed and chopped)

Sugar to taste - (start with 3 tablespoons)

Milk Powder-2 tablespoons

Green Cardamom (*Chhoti Elaichi*)–2 crushed

Saffron-few strands (optional)

Method

In a heavy bottomed wok, bring the milk to boil.

Add the chopped cauliflower.

Keep stirring on low heat making sure that NOTHING BURNS.

As the mixture begins to thicken, add the milk powder, sugar, the cardamom and the saffron.

Stir well and keep stirring for about 5 minutes.

Switch off the heat source.

That's all. Your delicious *Gobi ka Kheer* (Cauliflower Pudding) is ready.

You can let it cool down, then put it in the fridge and have it when it is cold.

Prep time: 5 minute

Cooking time: 20 minutes

Total time: 25 minutes

Lauki Ka Kheer (Bottle Gourd Pudding)

Ever imagined turning the humble, and rather tasteless, bottle gourd into a tasty dish? No, then read on.

Serves 3-4

Ingredients

Full cream milk-1 litre (2 US pints liquid) (4 cups)

Bottle Gourd-2 cup- 500 grams (grated)

Sugar to taste - (start with 3 tablespoons)

Milk Powder-6 tablespoons

Green Cardamom (*Chhoti Elaichi*)–2 crushed

Method

In a heavy bottomed wok, bring the milk to boil.

Add the grated bottle gourd.

Keep stirring on low heat making sure that NOTHING BURNS.

As the mixture begins to thicken (which will take some time as the bottle gourd releases a lot of water), add the milk powder, sugar, and the cardamom.

Stir well and keep stirring for about 5 minutes.

Switch off the heat source.

That's all. Your delicious *Lauki ka Kheer* (Bottle Gourd Pudding) is ready.

You can let it cool down, then put it in the fridge and have it when it is cold.

Prep time: 5 minute

Cooking time: 30 minutes

Total time: 35 minutes

Makhane Ka Kheer (Lotus Seed Pudding)

Makhana or lotus seeds, also called fox nut or gorgon nut, have been used extensively in traditional Oriental and Chinese medicine for their nutritional and healing properties. However, being low in fat and high in carbohydrates, these are nutritionally distinct from other nuts and seeds.

Lotus seeds are a good source of protein, carbohydrates, fibre, magnesium, potassium, phosphorus, iron and zinc. Their low sodium and high magnesium content makes them useful for those suffering from heart diseases, high blood pressure, diabetes and obesity.

You can eat them salted, like salted cashew nuts, or as a sweet pudding. We share the recipe for the latter here.

Serves 3-4

Ingredients

Full cream milk-1 litre (2 US pints liquid) (4 cups)

Lotus Seeds-1 cup- 250 grams

Sugar to taste - (start with 3 tablespoons)

Milk Powder-6 tablespoons

Green Cardamom (*Chhoti Elaichi*)-2 crushed

Method

Submerge the lotus seeds in a bowl of water for 2 minutes and then take out and squeeze out the water. Keep aside.

In a heavy bottomed wok, bring the milk to boil.

As the mixture begins to thicken, add the milk powder, sugar, and the cardamom.

Now add the lotus seeds.

Keep stirring on low heat making sure that NOTHING BURNS.

Stir well and keep stirring for about 5 minutes.

Switch off the heat source.

That's all. Your delicious *Makhane ka Kheer* (Lotus Seed Pudding) is ready.

You can either have it hot as some like it. Or you could let it cool down, then put it in the fridge and have it when it is cold.

Prep time: 5 minutes

Cooking time: 20 minutes

Total time: 25 minutes

Gajar Ka Kheer (Carrot Pudding)

Yet another version of the classic winter dessert that you will find in North India.

Serves 3-4

Ingredients

Full cream milk-1 litre (2 US pints liquid) (4 cups)

Carrot-1 cup- 250 grams (grated)

Sugar to taste - (start with 3 tablespoons)

Milk Powder-4 tablespoons

Green Cardamom (*Chhoti Elaichi*)-2 crushed

Method

In a heavy bottomed wok, bring the milk to boil.

Add the grated carrots.

Keep stirring on low heat making sure that NOTHING BURNS.

As the mixture begins to thicken, add the milk powder, sugar, and the cardamom.

Stir well and keep stirring for about 5 minutes.

Switch off the heat source.

That's all. Your delicious *Gajar ka Kheer* (Carrot Pudding) is ready.

You can let it cool down, then put it in the fridge and have it when it is cold.

Prep time: 5 minutes

Cooking time: 25 minutes

Total time: 30 minutes

Lauki Ki Barfi (Bottle Gourd Sweets)

Yet another way to turn the humble, and rather tasteless, bottle gourd into a tasty sweet meat.

Serves 3-4

Ingredients

Full cream milk-1 litre (2 US pints liquid) (4 cups)

Bottle Gourd-2 cup- 500 grams (grated)

Sugar - 1 cup

Milk Powder-6 tablespoons

Green Cardamom (*Chhoti Elaichi*)-2 crushed

Melon Seeds- 2 tablespoon (optional)

Ghee (Clarified butter) - 1 tea spoon

Method

In a heavy bottomed wok, bring the milk to boil.

As the mixture begins to thicken, add the milk powder.

Keep stirring on low heat making sure that NOTHING BURNS.

When the milk is totally reduced, switch off the heat source and keep aside.

In another vessel, add the sugar and put it on your heat source.

As soon as the sugar starts to melt, add the grated bottle gourd.

Stir well and keep stirring till the mixture starts drying.

Add the green cardamom.

Switch off the heat source.

Take a plate and coat it with the *ghee*.

Pour the bottle gourd mixture on it and flatten with a spoon.

Cover it evenly with the reduced milk.

Sprinkle over the melon seeds.

After it cools down, cut into squares.

That's all. Your delicious *Lauki ki Barfi* (Bottle Gourd Sweet) is ready.

Prep time: 5 minutes

Cooking time: 60 minutes

Total time: 65 minutes

***Chukandar Ka Halwa* (Beetroot Halwa)**

Inspired by the more popular *Gajar Halwa*, this one is a stunner visually because of its colour.

Serves 3-4

Ingredients

Full cream milk-2 litre (4 US pints liquid) (8 cups)

Beettroot-2 cup- 500 grams (peeled and grated)

Sugar to taste - (start with 5 tablespoons)

Milk Powder-6 tablespoons

Green Cardamom (*Chhoti Elaichi*)-3 crushed

Ghee (clarified butter) - 2 table spoons

Method

In a heavy bottomed wok, bring the milk to boil.

Add the grated beetroots.

Keep stirring on low heat making sure that NOTHING BURNS.

As the mixture begins to thicken, add the milk powder, and the cardamom.

Stir well and keep stirring till the mixture becomes almost dry.

Now add the sugar and keep stirring till all the sugar is melted and well blended.

Keep stirring till the mixture again becomes dry.

Now add the *ghee* and stir for five more minutes.

Switch off the heat source.

That's all. Your delicious *Chukandar ka Halwa* (Beetroot *Halwa*) is ready.

You can either have it hot as some like it. Or you could let it cool down, then put it in the fridge and have it when it is cold.

Prep time: 10 minutes

Cooking time: 60 minutes

Total time: 70 minutes

Chapter 7: BONUS on the Side

As mentioned, Indians everywhere like to enjoy their curries with simple boiled rice. Occasionally, with dry dishes, or with thicker curries, they may (especially in Punjab) try out *rotis* (the Indian unleavened bread).

No harm then, if I share the recipes for making simple rice and *roti* too in this book to turn this in to a complete Veggie Cookbook.

Rice Boiled

Ingredients

Rice-1 cup

Water-2 cups

Tip: Use the same cup please! Otherwise, your rice will NOT turn out to be fluffy.

Wash the rice well (in a vessel 3-4 times, but don't rub it lest the grains break) and let it naturally "dry", on an inclined plate, for 15-20 minutes. This helps enhance the aroma.

If you have a Rice Cooker, follow its instructions. Otherwise, I present three popular methods below to turn out a perfect plate of boiled rice.

Method using a pressure cooker

In a pressure cooker (3-5 litre capacity or 6-11 US pints capacity) bring the water to a boil.

Add the rice to the boiling water.

Close the lid of the pressure cooker BUT remove the weight.

When steam starts escaping from the vent (don't worry, you will hear that typical sound), reduce the heat to minimum. In other words, if cooking on gas, turn the knob to SIM (mer).

Wait for 10 minutes and switch off the gas. Take out the rice. Your hot fluffy rice is ready.

Method using a thick bottomed vessel/deep pan

In a vessel or a pan, bring the water to a boil.

Add the rice to the boiling water. Turn the heat to low and cover the vessel/deep pan with a well-fitting lid.

Cook for 15-20 minutes without stirring the rice. Switch off the heat source. Lift the lid and check whether the rice is properly cooked.

Cooked rice is always soft. To check, you have to take out a grain of rice and press it between your fingers (obviously use a spoon to take out the grain to avoid scalding your hands).

If the grain is still hard, that means it is under cooked. If it is soft, then it is cooked properly.

In case the grain is not properly cooked, you may like to add another ½ cup of water and let it cook on low heat for another 7-10 minutes.

Traditional method (the way it is cooked in villages or dhabas even today)

In a vessel or a pan, bring three (instead of two mentioned in the above two methods) cups of water (for one cup of rice) to a boil.

Add the rice to the boiling water. Turn the heat to medium and don't cover the vessel/deep pan, because the water will boil and spill over.

Cook for 15-20 minutes stirring the rice gently from time to time. Keep on checking whether the rice is properly cooked.

Once the rice is done, switch off the heat source. Drain all the excess water. (You can use a colander. Traditionally, the vessel will just be covered with a lid and the water poured out. This is tricky as both the vessel and the water would be very hot.)

Although the traditional method takes more time, it is believed to bring out the flavours better. Since the water used for boiling the rice is totally drained out, some dieticians claim that this method helps take out some of the starch from the rice thus shaving off some calories from this dish.

Tip: The drained out water can act as an excellent stock for soups especially when it comes out of the local red coloured rice.

Method using a rice cooker

Place the rice and water in the rice cooker.

Close the lid and switch on the cooker. The rice will be cooked and the rice cooker will switch off on its own.

This is the easiest and quite a fool proof way of making rice.

Prep time: 20 minutes

Cooking time: 10 minutes with a pressure cooker; 15-20 minutes with a deep pan; and as indicated in the rice cooker manual

Total time: 30 minutes with a pressure cooker; 35-40 minutes with a deep pan

(Excerpted from my book: The Ultimate Guide to Cooking Rice the Indian Way, which contains 34 more such rice dishes.)

The Classic Indian *Roti/Phulka/Chapati*

This simple Indian bread, free of yeast or any other leavening agent, is what many Indian homes have every day for lunch or dinner. It is surprising then that most restaurants don't have *chapatis* on their menus. Instead they focus on making Tandoori *Rotis* or Nans, which they probably find easier to handle when larger numbers are to be served.

For most households, however, it won't be easy to invest in a Tandoor (earthen oven). For them then it will have to be the simple, non-fussy *chapati*. And here's how you can go about making these.

Note: I have seen people rolling dough with a steel tumbler on any flat surface, or using just their hands to give dough the roundish shape of a *roti*. I think it prudent, however, for all newbies to invest in a rolling pin (*belan*) and rolling board (*chakla*) before attempting to make *chapatis*.

Ingredients

Whole Wheat Flour-3 cups (enough for 5 *chapatis*)

Luke Warm Water-1 cup

Method

In a mixing bowl, put 2 + ½ cups of flour, reserving ½ cup as *parthan* (dusting) for rolling out the *chapatis* later.

Add the water and make into a nice firm dough.

Shape the dough into balls about the size of a large walnut.

In another plate, put the remaining wheat flour (the reserved ½ cup), and press the ball into this dry flour.

At this point, take a thick griddle and put it on your heat source.

While the griddle heats up, take out your rolling board (*chakla*).

Using a rolling pin (*belan*), shape the dough ball (that is already rolled into the dry flour), into a small circular shape as thin as you can make it.

Now, on the heated griddle place this rolled out *chapati*.

Let it cook a little on one side and then flip over for the other side to also cook.

Using a tong, remove the *chapati* from the griddle and place it directly on the flame.

The *chapati* will immediately swell up and will be ready to be served.

In case you don't have a heat source with a flame, then you will have to puff up the *chapati* on the griddle itself. For this you will need a handkerchief with which you should gently press the edges of the

---

chapati as it swells on the griddle flipping it for a second time.

Prep time: 5 minutes

Cooking time: 5 minutes for 5 *chapatis* @1 minute per *chapati*

Total time: 10 minutes

(Excerpted from my book: Home Style Indian Cooking In A Jiffy, which contains over 100 exotic Indian recipes including for *Poori* and *Paratha*, the two most popular Indian unleavened bread dishes.)

Appendix: An Introduction to Some Basic Indian Spices and Ingredients

It is easy to be overwhelmed with the sheer number and variety of fresh herbs and spices that are commonly used in Indian cuisine. I shouldn't, therefore, make this topic even more complicated by giving the scientific or botanical names of such spices, or where they grow, or how these are harvested and processed. There are many excellent books who have done better justice to this topic.

What I shall attempt here is to just list out some twenty of these spices that you should experiment with when you are just starting out with "Home Style" Indian cooking. The ones in bold are essential for any authentic Indian kitchen. The rest are optional.

The discerning reader may notice the omission of *Kastoori Methi* (a very fragrant variety of Fenugreek) which is very popular for making curries in Indian restaurants. That's precisely the reason why I am leaving this out from my list.

But if you prefer your food to taste like *dhaba* food, do go ahead and stock on *Kastoori Methi* too. Just remember that this is such a strong herb that it will drown the fragrance of all other spices, howsoever expensive they may be.

So for heavens, don't use your saffron with *Kastoori Methi* ever!

I am also leaving out some expensive spices like nutmeg or star aniseed as they are hardly ever used in your day-to-day cooking.

Here is then my list, in alphabetical order.

Ajwain: *Ajwain* or *Ajowan* is pale brown in colour and looks somewhat like caraway or cumin. It has a bitter and pungent taste and its flavour is similar to anise and oregano. This spice smells almost exactly like thyme but is more aromatic and less subtle in taste. Even a small amount of *Ajwain* tends to dominate the flavour of a dish.

Amchur (Dried green mango powder): This is used for imparting a strong sour taste.

Asafoetida (Hing): This is used in small quantities for imparting a strong smell. It is considered very healthy for digestive purposes though some people may find the smell unpleasant and strong. Don't use your saffron with *Hing*, therefore, ever!

Cardamom (Elaichi): These come in two varieties: one is small, pale-green and the other is large and brown/black. The pale green variety is used in many Indian dishes including desserts. The brown variety is used for making curries or *pulaos*, but not in sweetmeats.

Chaat Masala: You should be able to get *Chaat Masala* from any Indian store. However, if you can't, you can make it at home by mixing together 1 teaspoon dried mango powder + 1 teaspoon rock salt + 1 teaspoon cumin powder + ½ teaspoon asafoetida + ½ teaspoon chilli powder.

Mix well and store in a dry jar for any use later on Indian snacks like *pakoras*.

Chilli (Kashmiri Red variety): In our recipes, we have suggested the use of Kashmiri Red Chillies as these impart a nice red colour and are not as hot as are the other red chillies. In case, you like your food to be really hot, then you can use the other red chillies available in the market which are much hotter.

Cinnamon (Dalchini): This looks like the thin bark of a tree and imparts a lovely flavour both to the sweet and curried dishes. In India, however, it is more used for curries as Indians like Cardamom in their desserts much more than Cinnamon.

Cloves (Laung): These look like dried flower buds and add a lovely flavour to the food. Cloves are supposed to have antiseptic qualities which helps preserve food.

Coconut (Nariyal) powder or milk: This is used commonly in many South Indian and coastal Indian preparations.

Coriander seeds and fresh green leaves (Dhania and Dhania patta): The dried seeds of Coriander form an essential part of Indian curries and are used quite extensively. The fresh green leaves are used for making chutneys (Indian sauce) as well as for sprinkling on curries. Since the fresh leaves have a strong flavour, they should only be used by those who really like the flavour.

Cumin seeds (Jeera): Cumin is another essential ingredient of Indian cuisine and is generally the first spice to go into the heated cooking oil before other items are added.

Curry leaves (Kare-patta): These leaves have a lovely flavour and are absolutely essential if you like South Indian cuisine. In India, it grows in abundance and so is easily the cheapest herb to use. Generally used fresh, these can also be dried and used as they retain much of their fragrance even in the dried form.

Fennel (Saunf): This is used for making some dishes and forms a part of the *Pach Phoran* (the Eastern Indian mixture of five spices).

Fenugreek (Methi): These are small flat seeds which have a slightly bitter flavour and must be used only in the quantities prescribed. They add quite a piquant flavour to the curries or dry dishes they are added to which is liked by many Indians.

Lately, fenugreek has acquired quite a cult status because of its almost magical effect in reducing the severity of diabetes.

Garam Masala: This is a mixture in equal quantities of cinnamon, cloves, cardamom (both pale-green and brown variety) and whole black pepper corns. These can be ground together and kept in air tight containers for future use for up to a week. Some dishes can also be made by putting the whole spices in oil/ clarified butter (*ghee*).

All lovers of Indian cooking must learn to use this mixture properly. If you cook Indian dishes only occasionally, you may be tempted to use the commercially available *garam masala* powders.

Please remember, however, that to economise on costs, some manufacturers skimp on the more expensive ingredients mentioned above and instead add lots of coriander powder, cumin powder, turmeric powder, red chilli powder etc. to add volume. They even add *kastoori methi* which just drowns the subtle flavours of other *garam masalas*.

So do check before you buy such a ready mix of spices.

Mustard seeds black (Rai): These are black mustard seeds which look the same as the yellow variety but are supposed to be more pungent than their yellow cousins. This mustard seed is used a lot in South Indian and Western Indian cooking.

Onion seeds dried (Mangrela or Kalonji): This spice is generally used as a part of the *Pach Phoran* (the Eastern Indian mixture of five spices).

Paneer: For those who don't know, *Paneer* is some kind of an uncured, fresh common cheese which is very popular in North Indian cuisine for savoury dishes and in East Indian cuisine for sweet meats. It is unlike any other cheese that I have tasted anywhere in the world.

Many of my non-Indian friends, when asked what they like best about Indian cuisine, have quoted *Paneer* recipes like *Mattar Paneer*, *Palak Paneer* or the Bengali sweet *Sandesh*.

However, if you don't live in India, you may have some difficulty finding ready-made *Paneer* in your local supermarket.

If that be so, you don't need to feel disheartened. I have a solution right here.

Here is how you can make *Paneer* easily at home and then go on to prepare your favourite sweet or savoury *Paneer* dish:

Ingredients

Whole Milk-1 litre (4 cups)

(If you wish to use toned or double-toned milk, you can, but you will then get less *paneer* in quantity.)

Fresh squeezed lemon juice-1 tablespoon

Method

Bring the milk to a full boil.

Add the lemon juice to the boiling milk. Stir well.

The milk will start curdling. Let it curdle fully.

Switch off the heat source.

Put a muslin cloth over a big colander, place this over a vessel and pour in it the curdled milk. The solids which remain on the muslin cloth is called *paneer*.

Let all the water drip from the *paneer*, for about an hour.

Cut the *paneer* into bite size pieces and use as you wish.

Enjoy!

Sambar Masala: Sambar masala would generally be available in Indian stores. However, to make it at home, add one tablespoon coriander powder + 2 teaspoon cumin powder + ½ teaspoon ground black pepper + ½ teaspoon chilli powder + ½ teaspoon turmeric powder + ¼ teaspoon asafoetida.

Mix well and store in a dry jar for any use later.

Turmeric (Haldi): This is easily the commonest and the most important ingredient in any Indian curry dish. Though it does not have much of a flavour, it has a dark yellow colour and a lot of therapeutic value.

Yoghurt (Dahi): Not really a spice or herb, yoghurt is frequently used in many Indian dishes. The variety used in cooking is cultured yoghurt and is always unflavoured. That way it comes closest to the Greek variety of yoghurt.

Please note that if you buy ready-made yoghurt from the supermarket, sometimes it splinters when you heat it.

If you so desire then, you can very easily make yoghurt at home using the following method:

First, to start the whole process, you will need to buy some unflavoured yoghurt. Subsequently about two tablespoons from the yoghurt you make can suffice to make the next home-made batch of yoghurt.

Ingredients

Milk-1 litre (4 cups)

Plain Unsweetened Yoghurt (as starter)-2 tablespoon

Method

Boil the milk well.

Tip: If you don't boil well, your yoghurt will set but will be a little sticky as factory-made yoghurts generally are.

Let the milk cool down to a level where it feels warm but not hot.

You should be able to use your finger for touching the milk without any fear of scalding it.

Beat the yoghurt well and gently add the warm milk.

Mix well.

Now pour this mixture into a bowl and place it in an insulated casserole.

I use an insulated lunch box which has a small heating element built-in. I need to "switch on" this lunch-box for about 30 minutes in really cold weather (where indoor temperatures be below 15 degree C or 59 degree F).

The basic idea is that the milk should remain warm for at least the next three hours.

After that the yoghurt sets on its own.

It is generally advisable to set the yoghurt at night so that you can have fresh yoghurt in the morning. This also ensures that the vessel is not moved during the entire period that the yoghurt is setting because movement spoils the setting.

Prep Time: 5 minutes

Setting Time: 5 hours (minimum three hours)

A Big Thank You for Reading This Book till the End

I'm indeed grateful that you chose MY BOOK.

I know you could have easily picked up any other book in this genre but am glad that you took a chance with mine. So a big THANKS for reposing your trust in me and reading this book all the way to the end.

If you liked this book, I shall be grateful if you could do me a small favour. Please take a moment to leave a review, on the eBook platform you bought it on, if you are happy.

If not, please tell me directly. Your feedback is of immense value to me as an Author.

Your suggestions will help me in writing the kind of books that you love.

"I hope this book will inspire the kitchen con-artist in you, increase fruit and veggie consumption in your family, and motivate you to become an Accidental Cook. Pass it on!"

— Merrin McGregor, Vegetables Accidentally: Healthier... But None the Wiser

Books by the Author in the "Cooking In A Jiffy" Series

HOME STYLE INDIAN COOKING IN A JIFFY

(Now available also in Italian, Japanese and Spanish)

Amazon #1 Best Seller in Indian and Professional Cooking

With an amazing compilation of over 100 delectable Indian dishes, many of which you can't get in any Indian restaurant for love or for money, this is unlike any other Indian Cook book. What this book focuses on is what Indians eat every day in their homes. It then in a step-by-step manner makes this mysterious, never disclosed, "Home Style" Indian cooking accessible to anyone with a rudimentary knowledge of cooking and a stomach for adventure.

To know more, do please go to:

https://authormarketing.booklaunch.io/prasenjeetk
umar@hotmail.com/home-style-indian-cooking-in-
a-jiffy

HOW TO COOK IN A JIFFY EVEN IF YOU HAVE
NEVER BOILED AN EGG BEFORE

(Now available also in Italian, German and
Portuguese)

Never boiled an egg before but want to learn the
magic art of cooking? Then don't leave home without
this Survival Cookbook.

Be it healthy college cooking, or cooking for a single
person or even outdoor cooking—this book helps you
survive all situations by teaching you how to cook
literally in a jiffy.

To know more, do please go to:

https://authormarketing.booklaunch.io/prasenjeetk
umar@hotmail.com/how-to-cook-in-a-jiffy

HEALTHY COOKING IN A JIFFY: THE COMPLETE
NO FAD NO DIET HANDBOOK

(Now available also in Portuguese and Spanish)

Amazon #1 in Hot New Releases in Health, Fitness &
Dieting> Special Diets> Healthy

Amazon #3 Best Seller in Health, Fitness & Dieting>
Special Diets> Healthy

If you are sick of dieting, counting calories, or gorging on supplements, do consider investing in this book of simply sensible cooking and get on to a journey of eternal joy and happiness.

To know more, do please go to:

https://authormarketing.booklaunch.io/prasenjeetk umar@hotmail.com/healthy-cooking-in-a-jiffy

THE ULTIMATE GUIDE TO COOKING LENTILS THE INDIAN WAY

(Now available also in German)

Amazon #1 Best Seller in Indian Cooking and Rice & Grains

Presenting 58 Tastiest Ways to Cook Lentils as Soups, Curries, Snacks, Full Meals and hold your breath, Desserts! As only Indians can.

To know more, do please go to:

https://authormarketing.booklaunch.io/prasenjeetk umar@hotmail.com/lentils-cookbook

THE ULTIMATE GUIDE TO COOKING RICE THE INDIAN WAY

Amazon #1 in Hot New Releases in Rice & Grains

From a Bed for Curries, to Pilaf, Biryani, Khichdi, Idli, Dosa, Savouries and Desserts, No One Cooks Rice as Lovingly as the Indians Do.

To know more, do please go to:

https://authormarketing.booklaunch.io/prasenjeetk umar@hotmail.com/the-ultimate-guide-to-cooking-rice-the-indian-way

THE ULTIMATE GUIDE TO COOKING FISH THE INDIAN WAY

43 Mouth-watering Ways to Cooking Fish in a JIFFY as Only Indians Can.

So say bye to the boring boiled and broiled ways to make fish and prawn dishes and let this new book open your eyes to the wonderful possibilities of cooking fish the way northern, southern, eastern and western Indians do.

There are six starter (or dry) dishes, 14 curries, 12 prawn dishes, and 4 ways to cook fish head and eggs (caviar) the Indian way.

For the spice-challenged or nostalgia ridden folks, there are 7 dishes from the days of the British Raj.

So if you were wondering how to incorporate this superb, dripping with long strands of polyunsaturated essential omega-3 fatty acids (that the human body can't naturally produce), low-calorie, high quality protein rich white meat in your daily diet, just grab this book with both your hands.

To know more, do please go to:

https://authormarketing.booklaunch.io/prasenjeetk
umar@hotmail.com/the-ultimate-guide-to-cooking-
fish-the-indian-way

THE ULTIMATE GUIDE TO COOKING CHICKEN THE INDIAN WAY

51 mouth-watering "Home-Style" ways to cooking chicken in a JIFFY as only Indians Can

From Prasenjeet Kumar, the #1 best-selling author of the "Cooking In A Jiffy" series of cookbooks, comes the absolutely Ultimate Guide to Cooking Chicken with such exotic spices and taste that you will be left asking for more.

You will learn to cook chicken with yoghurt and coconut milk, mustard and turmeric, curry leaves and *garam masala* (literally hot spices) and so on.

There are 7 starter (or snack) dishes, 8 dry recipes, 15 chicken curries, 5 recipes for cooking chicken with rice, and 8 ways to cook eggs THE INDIAN WAY.

For the spice-challenged or nostalgia ridden folks, there are 8 dishes from the days of the British Raj that do use cheese and involve baking, if you were missing that!

To know more, do please go to:

https://booklaunch.io/prasenjeetkumar@hotmail.c
om/chicken-indian-way

Books by the Author in the Romance Genre

LEGALLY IN LOVE (Book 1 in the Romance in India Series)

Meet Amit Verma, a 27 year-old dreamy corporate lawyer looking for a job in Delhi, India.

One morning, while going through his mobile phone contact list, he comes across the entry for Naina Karnad, a girl who stole his heart some two years back in his former workplace.

The problem: He has not dialled her number in a year.

Will they ever meet again?

Will their love life survive the corporate intrigues and the recession?

"Legally in love" is a powerful tale of two souls battling their way through the ruthless world of corporate office politics to discovering their true love and passion.

To know more, do please go to:

https://booklaunch.io/prasenjeetkumar@hotmail.com/legally-in-love

LOVE KARMA CROSSED (Book 2 in Romance in India Series)

He vowed he'd love her so much that even death will be scared to come near her…..

MUMBAI: Raj Sharma, an aspiring Bollywood actor, is devastated when he learns that his wife, Nisha, a celebrity singer and a woman he deeply loves, is terminally ill.

Nobody can save her.

Not modern or ancient medicine.

Not prayers or religious mumbo-jumbo.

Not soothsayers or evil eye totems—nothing works.

Raj believes only his love can save Nisha.

Others think that is irrational stupidity.

Who is right?

Will Raj succeed?

Or will the inevitable happen?

And will Raj be forced to helplessly watch his lovely wife die bit by bit in front of his eyes?

Strangely Raj and Nisha decide to embark on a journey. A life changing journey.

From the glittering lights of Hong Kong to the intriguing caves, ruins, churches and mosques of Turkey, the journey unravels the deepest mysteries of the human heart.

And always posing the question—whether love can really heal?

To know more, do please go to:

https://booklaunch.io/prasenjeetkumar@hotmail.com/love-karma-crossed

Books by the Author in the "Quiet Phoenix" Series

CELEBRATING QUIET PEOPLE: UPLIFTING STORIES FOR INTROVERTS AND HIGHLY SENSITIVE PERSONS

(Now available also in Portuguese, Italian and Spanish.)

Celebrating Quiet People: A unique collection of motivational, inspirational and uplifting TRUE stories for introverts and highly sensitive persons that you shouldn't miss....

From the Amazon #1 best-selling author of the "Quiet Phoenix" series of books comes an outstanding collection of biographies and events that guarantee to increase your self-compassion and self-esteem, regardless of your age, gender or status in society.

To know more, do please go to:

https://booklaunch.io/prasenjeetkumar@hotmail.com/cqp-priced

QUIET PHOENIX: AN INTROVERT'S GUIDE TO RISING IN CAREER & LIFE

(Now available also in Italian, Portuguese and Spanish.)

Amazon #1 Best Seller in Legal Profession and Ethics & Professional Responsibility

Like the legendary Phoenix bird rising from the ashes, "Quiet Phoenix" is an incredible career change story that Prasenjeet Kumar shares, with wit and charm, of the journey from being a Corporate Lawyer to becoming a Full Time Author-Entrepreneur using his introversion as a strength to overcome all obstacles.

To know more, do please go to:

https://authormarketing.booklaunch.io/prasenjeetkumar@hotmail.com/quietphoenix

QUIET PHOENIX 2: FROM FAILURE TO FULFILMENT: A MEMOIR OF AN INTROVERTED CHILD

(Now available also in Japanese.)

Amazon #1 Hot New Releases in Biographies & Memoirs > Professional and Academics > Educators

Celebrating The Quiet Child: A Must Read For every Parent, Teacher, Mentor, Sports Coach.........

Based on the author's own childhood experiences, the underlying theme of the book is that just as a Phoenix Bird is hardwired to be reborn from the ashes of her ancestors, her tears are meant to cure wounds and the way she symbolises undying hope and optimism, so is your Quiet Child built for persistence, creativity, and self-discipline. She will also, without any goading, display a knack for self-learning, high emotional intelligence and an impeccable sense of moral responsibility. So nurture and celebrate that Quiet Child.

To know more, do please go to:

https://authormarketing.booklaunch.io/prasenjeetk umar@hotmail.com/quietphoenix2-priced

CELEBRATING QUIET LEADERS: UPLIFTING STORIES OF INTROVERTED LEADERS WHO CHANGED HISTORY

(Now available also in Portuguese and Spanish)

What do you think is common between George Washington and the Buddha, Mustafa Kemal Atatürk and Nelson Mandela, Rosa Parks and Florence Nightingale.........

That they were great leaders?

True. But did you know that they were also all introverts?

From Prasenjeet Kumar, the Amazon #1 best-selling author, comes an outstanding collection of uplifting stories of the greatest leaders of all times that have used their powers of introversion to rewrite History.

Most importantly, these leaders succeeded not because they could overcome their introversion, BUT because of their gifted strengths of introversion.

So, ladies and gentlemen, be prepared to immerse yourselves into legendary tales of courage and valour shown by quiet, shy and sensitive men and women from all around the world.

To know more, do please go to:

https://booklaunch.io/prasenjeetkumar@hotmail.com/celebrating-quiet-leaders

CELEBRATING QUIET ARTISTS: STIRRING STORIES OF INTROVERTED ARTISTS WHO THE WORLD CAN'T FORGET

Finally a Book that Celebrates the Creativity and Rich Imagination of Introverts

Do you really think legends like Steven Spielberg, Agatha Christie, J.K. Rowling, Leonardo Da Vinci, Amitabh Bachchan and the like were extroverted and outgoing— unlike you?

No. Absolutely wrong.

They were quiet. And introverts. Like me. Like you. And yet, their contribution is so well known.

Just imagine a world WITHOUT them. What would it be like? Without Harry Potter. Without Mona Lisa. Without Hercule Poirot. Without Inspector Vijay. Without E.T.

So if these artists were really introverts like you and me, how did they leave such an indelible imprint on this world?

Did they learn to become fake extroverts? Did they practise skills of socialising? Did they learn to talk non-stop?

Hell no.

They stayed true to themselves.

Puzzled? Then grab a copy today!

And enjoy many refreshing stories of introverted artists who used their god gifted strengths of introversion to overcome heart-breaking tragedies, challenges, and setbacks.

To know more, do please go to:

https://booklaunch.io/prasenjeetkumar@hotmail.com/celebrating-quiet-artists

Books by the Author in the "Self-Publishing WITHOUT SPENDING A DIME" Series

HOW TO BE AN AUTHOR ENTREPRENEUR WITHOUT SPENDING A DIME

(Now Available also in Spanish and Italian)

Are you making the same costly mistakes that Authors usually make?

If that be so, then here is a book that can help realise your author-entrepreneur dreams WITHOUT SPENDING A DIME.

This book contains everything you need to know about self-publishing and also contains a list of helpful video tutorials and resources.

Here is the link:

https://booklaunch.io/prasenjeetkumar@hotmail.c
om/author-entrepreneur-priced

HOW TO TRANSLATE YOUR BOOKS WITHOUT SPENDING A DIME

(Now Available also in Portuguese and Italian)

Enca$h the power of translation WITHOUT SPENDING A DIME.

Remember Paulo Coelho's "The Alchemist"? Could it be setting a Guinness World Record if it had not sold more than 65 million copies in 67 different languages?

So if you too could translate your bestseller FROM ENGLISH INTO DIFFERENT WORLD LANGUAGES, it could mean reaching such newer, untapped, unexplored markets whose existence you were blissfully unaware of.

Interested? Then grab this DIY manual of practical tips and advice that can take your writing dreams to literally translation Nirvana.

To know more, do please go to:

https://booklaunch.io/prasenjeetkumar@hotmail.c
om/how-to-translate-priced

HOW TO MARKET YOUR BOOKS WITHOUT SPENDING A DIME

Finally a Book on Marketing that cuts out the Fluff and Focuses only on the ESSENTIALS.

Are you bombarded with strange and esoteric marketing advice, to sell your books in 1000 ways, that leaves you baffled, bewildered and terribly confused?

Do you feel that learning and mastering those complicated strategies have sucked away all the joy you once had for writing?

Then this book focusing on the BARE ESSENTIALS for marketing your book may just be what the doctor ordered.

From Prasenjeet Kumar, the Amazon #1 Best Selling Author of "Self-Publishing WITHOUT SPENDING A DIME" series of books, comes a book that after discussing all the fluff and jargon that marketing gurus spout establishes why

less is always more.

At last!

To know more, do please go to:

https://booklaunch.io/prasenjeetkumar@hotmail.com/how-to-market

Connect With the Author

Feel free to visit me at: http://www.publishwithprasen.com

Should you have any questions or comments, or desire to collaborate with me on any future project, please do not hesitate to write to me anytime at prasenjeet@publishwithprasen.com

I am definitely looking for partners for carrying the "Cooking In A JIFFY" series forward to cover it by national/regional cuisines.

So if you are game to do, say "Home Style German/Italian/Chinese/Japanese.... Cooking In A JIFFY" with me, do please get in touch.

I would also love to connect with you on Social Media. Join me on:

Twitter

https://twitter.com/PublishWithPras

Goodreads

https://www.goodreads.com/prasenjeet

Google Plus

https://www.google.com/+PrasenjeetKumarAuthor

About The Authors

Prasenjeet Kumar

Prasenjeet Kumar is the author of over 18 books in four genres: Fiction-Romance, motivational books for introverts (the Quiet Phoenix series), books on Self-Publishing (Self-Publishing Without Spending a Dime series) and cookbooks (Cooking In A Jiffy series). His books (23 titles so far) have also been translated into German, Italian, Japanese, Spanish, and Portuguese.

Prasenjeet is a Law graduate from the University College London (2005-2008), London University and a Philosophy Honours graduate from St. Stephen's College (2002-2005), Delhi University. In addition, he holds a Legal Practice Course (LPC) Diploma from College of Law, Bloomsbury, London.

Prasenjeet loves gourmet food, music, films, golf and travelling. He has already covered seventeen countries including Canada, China, Denmark, Dubai, Germany, Hong Kong, Indonesia, Macau, Malaysia, Sharjah, Sweden, Switzerland, Thailand, Turkey, UK, Uzbekistan, and the USA.

Prasenjeet is the self-taught designer, writer, editor and proud owner of the website cookinginajiffy.com which he has dedicated to his mother. He also runs another website publishwithprasen.com where he shares tips about writing and self-publishing.

Sonali Kumar

Sonali Kumar retired from the Indian Administrative Service (IAS) after a distinguished service of over 36 years with the Government of India as well as the Government of Jammu and Kashmir.

During this period, she held a number of assignments related to industry and commerce (including Public Sector Undertakings), textiles (handlooms & handicrafts), education, welfare, forests & environment, agriculture, horticulture, co-operatives, rural and urban development, health & medical education, anti-drought prone and anti-desert area development programmes, revenue, judicial, and even disaster relief operations.

Sonali believes that her myriad experiences spanning all kinds of sectors have equipped her with the powers of ideation, problem-solving, out-of-box thinking, and strategic policy insights that only a long stint in IAS probably can endow one with.

Post-retirement, Sonali is working with her son Prasenjeet putting out books in the "Cooking In A Jiffy" series. In her spare time, she doesn't mind mentoring or advising people who wish to benefit from other otherwise vast experience in public service.

Index